50 Thai Iced Tea and Dessert Recipes for Home

By: Kelly Johnson

Table of Contents

- Thai Iced Tea
- Thai Tea Pudding
- Thai Tea Ice Cream
- Thai Tea Panna Cotta
- Thai Tea Tiramisu
- Thai Tea Cheesecake
- Thai Tea Macarons
- Thai Tea Cupcakes
- Thai Tea Crème Brûlée
- Thai Tea Mousse
- Thai Tea Flan
- Thai Tea Cake Roll
- Thai Tea Cookies
- Thai Tea Milkshake
- Thai Tea Latte
- Thai Tea Sorbet
- Thai Tea Granita
- Thai Tea Truffles
- Thai Tea Marshmallows
- Thai Tea Soufflé
- Thai Tea Crepes
- Thai Tea Bread Pudding
- Thai Tea Tapioca Pudding
- Thai Tea Rice Krispie Treats
- Thai Tea Coconut Rice
- Thai Tea Chia Pudding
- Thai Tea Pound Cake
- Thai Tea Scones
- Thai Tea Parfait
- Thai Tea Ice Pops
- Thai Tea Popsicles
- Thai Tea Smoothie
- Thai Tea Jelly
- Thai Tea Custard Tart
- Thai Tea Rice Balls

- Thai Tea Shortbread
- Thai Tea Waffles
- Thai Tea Donuts
- Thai Tea Pancakes
- Thai Tea Caramel Sauce
- Thai Tea Tres Leches Cake
- Thai Tea Layer Cake
- Thai Tea Pecan Pie
- Thai Tea Bundt Cake
- Thai Tea Fudge
- Thai Tea Baklava
- Thai Tea Éclair
- Thai Tea Biscotti
- Thai Tea Crêpes Suzette
- Thai Tea Brulee Cheesecake

Thai Iced Tea

Ingredients:

- 4 cups water
- 4 Thai tea bags (or black tea bags)
- 1/2 cup sweetened condensed milk
- Ice cubes
- Optional: additional sweetener (such as sugar or honey), evaporated milk, or coconut milk

Instructions:

Bring the water to a boil in a saucepan.
Once boiling, remove the saucepan from the heat and add the Thai tea bags (or black tea bags). Let the tea steep for about 5-10 minutes, depending on how strong you like your tea.
After steeping, remove the tea bags and discard them.
Let the brewed tea cool to room temperature, then transfer it to a pitcher or container and refrigerate until cold.
To serve, fill glasses with ice cubes and pour the cold brewed tea over the ice, leaving some space at the top of each glass.
Drizzle about 2 tablespoons of sweetened condensed milk over each glass of tea. Stir gently to combine.
Taste the Thai Iced Tea and adjust the sweetness to your liking by adding more sweetened condensed milk or additional sweetener if desired.
Optionally, you can also add a splash of evaporated milk or coconut milk for extra creaminess.
Serve the Thai Iced Tea immediately and enjoy its deliciously unique flavor!

Thai Iced Tea is perfect for hot summer days or as a refreshing beverage any time of the year. Its combination of bold tea flavors and creamy sweetness makes it a favorite among tea lovers everywhere.

Thai Tea Pudding

Ingredients:

- 2 cups brewed Thai tea (prepared with Thai tea leaves or Thai tea bags)
- 1 cup whole milk
- 1/2 cup sweetened condensed milk
- 1/4 cup granulated sugar (adjust to taste)
- 1/4 cup cornstarch
- 1/4 cup cold water
- 1 teaspoon vanilla extract
- Optional: toasted coconut flakes or chopped nuts for garnish

Instructions:

In a saucepan, combine the brewed Thai tea, whole milk, sweetened condensed milk, and granulated sugar. Heat the mixture over medium heat until it starts to simmer, stirring occasionally to dissolve the sugar. Once simmering, reduce the heat to low and let it steep for about 5 minutes to infuse the flavors.
In a small bowl, whisk together the cornstarch and cold water until smooth, creating a slurry.
Slowly pour the cornstarch slurry into the simmering Thai tea mixture, whisking constantly to prevent lumps from forming.
Cook the mixture over low heat, stirring constantly, until it thickens to a pudding-like consistency, about 5-7 minutes.
Once thickened, remove the pudding from the heat and stir in the vanilla extract.
Pour the pudding into serving dishes or ramekins. You can strain the pudding through a fine-mesh sieve if you prefer a smoother texture.
Let the pudding cool to room temperature, then cover and refrigerate for at least 2 hours, or until chilled and set.
Before serving, garnish the Thai Tea Pudding with toasted coconut flakes or chopped nuts if desired.
Serve and enjoy this creamy and flavorful Thai Tea Pudding as a delightful dessert!

This Thai Tea Pudding is a wonderful way to enjoy the unique and aromatic flavors of Thai tea in a creamy and comforting dessert. It's perfect for special occasions or as a sweet treat to indulge in any time of the day.

Thai Tea Ice Cream

Ingredients:

- 2 cups heavy cream
- 1 cup whole milk
- 1/2 cup sweetened condensed milk
- 1/2 cup granulated sugar
- 1/4 cup Thai tea leaves or 4-5 Thai tea bags
- 5 large egg yolks
- 1 teaspoon vanilla extract
- Optional: chopped toasted nuts or sweetened condensed milk for topping

Instructions:

In a saucepan, combine the heavy cream, whole milk, sweetened condensed milk, and granulated sugar. Heat the mixture over medium heat, stirring occasionally, until it begins to simmer. Once simmering, remove the saucepan from the heat. Add the Thai tea leaves or Thai tea bags to the hot cream mixture, stirring to submerge them completely. Let the mixture steep for about 30 minutes to infuse the flavors of the tea.

After steeping, strain the mixture through a fine-mesh sieve to remove the tea leaves or tea bags, pressing down gently to extract as much liquid as possible. Discard the tea leaves or tea bags.

Return the strained mixture to the saucepan and reheat over medium heat until it is hot but not boiling.

In a separate bowl, whisk the egg yolks until smooth.

Gradually pour a small amount of the hot cream mixture into the egg yolks, whisking constantly, to temper the eggs. Continue adding the hot cream mixture slowly, whisking constantly, until all of the cream mixture has been incorporated into the egg yolks.

Pour the mixture back into the saucepan and cook over medium heat, stirring constantly with a wooden spoon or heatproof spatula, until the mixture thickens and coats the back of the spoon, about 5-7 minutes. Do not let it boil.

Remove the saucepan from the heat and stir in the vanilla extract.

Strain the mixture through a fine-mesh sieve into a clean bowl to remove any lumps or bits of cooked egg.

Cover the bowl with plastic wrap, pressing it directly onto the surface of the mixture to prevent a skin from forming. Chill the mixture in the refrigerator for at least 4 hours, or until completely cold.

Once chilled, transfer the mixture to an ice cream maker and churn according to the manufacturer's instructions until it reaches a soft-serve consistency.

Transfer the churned ice cream to a freezer-safe container and freeze for an additional 4 hours, or until firm.

Serve the Thai Tea Ice Cream scooped into bowls or cones, topped with chopped toasted nuts or a drizzle of sweetened condensed milk if desired.

Enjoy this creamy and flavorful homemade Thai Tea Ice Cream as a refreshing dessert!

Thai Tea Panna Cotta

Ingredients:

- 1 cup heavy cream
- 1 cup whole milk
- 1/4 cup granulated sugar
- 2 tablespoons Thai tea leaves or 2 Thai tea bags
- 2 teaspoons unflavored gelatin
- 2 tablespoons cold water
- 1 teaspoon vanilla extract
- Optional: sweetened condensed milk or coconut milk for topping

Instructions:

In a saucepan, combine the heavy cream, whole milk, and granulated sugar. Heat the mixture over medium heat, stirring occasionally, until it begins to simmer. Once simmering, add the Thai tea leaves or Thai tea bags to the hot cream mixture, stirring to submerge them completely. Let the mixture steep for about 20-30 minutes to infuse the flavors of the tea.

After steeping, strain the mixture through a fine-mesh sieve to remove the tea leaves or tea bags, pressing down gently to extract as much liquid as possible. Discard the tea leaves or tea bags.

In a small bowl, sprinkle the gelatin over the cold water and let it sit for about 5 minutes to soften.

After the gelatin has softened, heat it in the microwave for about 10-15 seconds, or until it has completely dissolved. Be careful not to let it boil.

Add the dissolved gelatin to the strained cream mixture and whisk until well combined.

Stir in the vanilla extract.

Divide the mixture evenly among serving glasses or ramekins.

Refrigerate the panna cotta for at least 4 hours, or until set.

Once set, serve the Thai Tea Panna Cotta chilled, topped with a drizzle of sweetened condensed milk or coconut milk if desired.

Enjoy this creamy and flavorful Thai Tea Panna Cotta as a delicious dessert!

This Thai Tea Panna Cotta is a delightful way to enjoy the unique flavors of Thai tea in a creamy and elegant dessert. It's perfect for special occasions or as a sweet treat to indulge in any time of the day.

Thai Tea Tiramisu

Ingredients:

- 1 cup brewed Thai tea, cooled to room temperature
- 1 cup heavy cream
- 1/2 cup granulated sugar, divided
- 8 ounces mascarpone cheese, softened
- 1 teaspoon vanilla extract
- 24 ladyfinger cookies (savoiardi)
- Cocoa powder, for dusting
- Optional: chopped toasted nuts or shaved chocolate for garnish

Instructions:

In a shallow dish, combine the brewed Thai tea with 1/4 cup of granulated sugar. Stir until the sugar is dissolved. Set aside.

In a mixing bowl, beat the heavy cream with the remaining 1/4 cup of granulated sugar until stiff peaks form.

In another mixing bowl, whisk the mascarpone cheese until smooth. Stir in the vanilla extract.

Gently fold the whipped cream into the mascarpone mixture until well combined and smooth.

Dip each ladyfinger cookie into the brewed Thai tea mixture, turning to coat both sides briefly. Be careful not to soak the cookies too long, as they will become too soft.

Arrange a layer of dipped ladyfinger cookies in the bottom of a serving dish or an 8x8-inch baking dish, breaking them into pieces if necessary to fit.

Spread half of the mascarpone mixture over the layer of ladyfinger cookies, smoothing it out with a spatula.

Repeat the process with another layer of dipped ladyfinger cookies and the remaining mascarpone mixture.

Cover the dish with plastic wrap and refrigerate the Thai Tea Tiramisu for at least 4 hours, or preferably overnight, to allow the flavors to meld and the dessert to set.

Before serving, dust the top of the Tiramisu with cocoa powder using a fine-mesh sieve.

Optionally, garnish with chopped toasted nuts or shaved chocolate for added texture and flavor.
Serve the Thai Tea Tiramisu chilled and enjoy this deliciously unique twist on a classic dessert!

This Thai Tea Tiramisu is a delightful combination of creamy mascarpone cheese, delicate ladyfinger cookies, and the distinctive flavors of Thai tea. It's perfect for special occasions or as a sweet treat to indulge in any time of the day.

Thai Tea Cheesecake

Ingredients:

For the Crust:

- 1 1/2 cups graham cracker crumbs
- 1/4 cup granulated sugar
- 6 tablespoons unsalted butter, melted

For the Filling:

- 24 ounces (3 packages) cream cheese, softened
- 1 cup granulated sugar
- 3 tablespoons all-purpose flour
- 1 cup Thai tea, brewed and cooled to room temperature
- 4 large eggs
- 1 teaspoon vanilla extract

For the Topping (Optional):

- Whipped cream
- Crushed graham crackers
- Thai tea leaves for garnish

Instructions:

Preheat your oven to 325°F (160°C). Grease a 9-inch springform pan with butter or non-stick cooking spray.
In a mixing bowl, combine the graham cracker crumbs, granulated sugar, and melted butter for the crust. Mix until well combined.
Press the crumb mixture evenly into the bottom of the prepared springform pan. Use the bottom of a glass or measuring cup to press the mixture firmly.
Bake the crust in the preheated oven for 10 minutes. Remove from the oven and let it cool while you prepare the filling.
In a large mixing bowl, beat the softened cream cheese, granulated sugar, and flour together until smooth and creamy.

Gradually add the brewed Thai tea to the cream cheese mixture, beating until well incorporated.

Add the eggs one at a time, beating well after each addition. Mix in the vanilla extract until smooth.

Pour the filling over the cooled crust in the springform pan, spreading it out evenly.

Tap the pan gently on the counter to release any air bubbles.

Place the springform pan in a larger baking dish and fill the larger dish with hot water until it comes halfway up the sides of the springform pan. This water bath will help prevent the cheesecake from cracking.

Bake the cheesecake in the preheated oven for 55-60 minutes, or until the edges are set and the center is slightly jiggly.

Turn off the oven and leave the cheesecake inside with the door closed for 1 hour to cool gradually.

Remove the cheesecake from the oven and let it cool completely at room temperature.

Once cooled, refrigerate the cheesecake for at least 4 hours, or overnight, to chill and set completely.

Before serving, you can top the cheesecake with whipped cream, crushed graham crackers, and Thai tea leaves for garnish if desired.

Slice and serve the Thai Tea Cheesecake chilled, and enjoy the creamy texture and unique flavors!

This Thai Tea Cheesecake is a delightful twist on the classic dessert, with the aromatic flavors of Thai tea infusing every creamy bite. It's perfect for special occasions or as a sweet treat to enjoy any time of the year.

Thai Tea Macarons

Ingredients:

For the Macaron Shells:

- 1 cup almond flour
- 1 3/4 cups powdered sugar
- 3 large egg whites, at room temperature
- 1/4 cup granulated sugar
- 1 tablespoon Thai tea leaves (finely ground)

For the Thai Tea Ganache Filling:

- 1/2 cup heavy cream
- 2 tablespoons Thai tea leaves
- 6 ounces white chocolate, finely chopped
- 1 tablespoon unsalted butter, softened

Instructions:

1. Prepare the Thai Tea Ganache Filling:

- In a small saucepan, heat the heavy cream over medium heat until it just begins to simmer.
- Remove the cream from the heat and add the Thai tea leaves. Let steep for about 10 minutes.
- Strain the cream through a fine-mesh sieve to remove the tea leaves.
- Return the strained cream to the saucepan and heat it again until it starts to simmer.
- Place the chopped white chocolate in a heatproof bowl. Pour the hot cream over the chocolate and let it sit for 1-2 minutes.
- Gently stir the mixture until the chocolate is melted and smooth.
- Add the softened butter to the ganache and stir until well combined.
- Cover the bowl with plastic wrap, pressing it directly onto the surface of the ganache to prevent a skin from forming. Refrigerate the ganache until firm, about 2 hours.

2. Make the Macaron Shells:

- Preheat your oven to 300°F (150°C). Line baking sheets with parchment paper or silicone baking mats.
- In a food processor, pulse together the almond flour, powdered sugar, and finely ground Thai tea leaves until well combined and fine in texture.
- In a clean, dry mixing bowl, beat the egg whites on medium speed until foamy.
- Gradually add the granulated sugar to the egg whites while continuing to beat. Increase the speed to high and beat until stiff, glossy peaks form.
- Gently fold the almond flour mixture into the beaten egg whites until just combined and smooth. Be careful not to overmix.
- Transfer the macaron batter to a piping bag fitted with a round tip.
- Pipe small circles of batter onto the prepared baking sheets, spacing them about 1 inch apart.
- Tap the baking sheets on the counter a few times to release any air bubbles.
- Let the piped macarons sit at room temperature for about 30 minutes, or until a thin skin forms on the surface.
- Bake the macarons in the preheated oven for 15-18 minutes, or until the shells are set and the tops are firm to the touch.
- Remove the macarons from the oven and let them cool completely on the baking sheets before gently peeling them off.

3. Assemble the Macarons:

- Match the cooled macaron shells into pairs of similar size.
- Transfer the chilled Thai tea ganache filling to a piping bag fitted with a round tip.
- Pipe a small amount of ganache onto the flat side of one macaron shell in each pair.
- Sandwich the filled shell with another shell, pressing down gently to distribute the filling evenly.
- Repeat with the remaining macaron shells and filling.
- Place the assembled macarons in an airtight container and refrigerate them for at least 24 hours to allow the flavors to meld and the texture to soften.
- Bring the macarons to room temperature before serving, and enjoy the delicious Thai Tea Macarons!

These Thai Tea Macarons are delicate, flavorful, and perfect for any special occasion or as a unique treat to enjoy with friends and family.

Thai Tea Cupcakes

Ingredients:

For the Cupcakes:

- 1 1/2 cups all-purpose flour
- 1 1/2 teaspoons baking powder
- 1/4 teaspoon salt
- 2 tablespoons Thai tea leaves (finely ground)
- 1/2 cup unsalted butter, softened
- 1 cup granulated sugar
- 2 large eggs, at room temperature
- 1 teaspoon vanilla extract
- 1/2 cup whole milk

For the Frosting:

- 1/2 cup unsalted butter, softened
- 2 cups powdered sugar
- 2 tablespoons Thai tea concentrate (brewed Thai tea, cooled to room temperature and strained)
- 1 teaspoon vanilla extract
- Pinch of salt

Instructions:

1. Make the Cupcakes:

- Preheat your oven to 350°F (175°C). Line a muffin tin with cupcake liners.
- In a mixing bowl, whisk together the all-purpose flour, baking powder, salt, and finely ground Thai tea leaves.
- In another mixing bowl, cream together the softened butter and granulated sugar until light and fluffy.
- Beat in the eggs one at a time, followed by the vanilla extract.
- Gradually add the dry ingredients to the wet ingredients, alternating with the whole milk, and mixing until just combined.

- Divide the batter evenly among the prepared cupcake liners, filling each about 2/3 full.
- Bake the cupcakes in the preheated oven for 18-20 minutes, or until a toothpick inserted into the center comes out clean.
- Remove the cupcakes from the oven and let them cool in the muffin tin for a few minutes before transferring them to a wire rack to cool completely.

2. Make the Frosting:

- In a mixing bowl, beat the softened butter until smooth and creamy.
- Gradually add the powdered sugar, one cup at a time, and beat until well combined and fluffy.
- Add the Thai tea concentrate, vanilla extract, and a pinch of salt, and beat until smooth and creamy.
- If the frosting is too thick, you can add a little more Thai tea concentrate or milk to reach your desired consistency.

3. Frost the Cupcakes:

- Once the cupcakes have cooled completely, use a piping bag fitted with a decorating tip to pipe the frosting onto the cupcakes.
- Alternatively, you can spread the frosting onto the cupcakes using a knife or offset spatula.
- Optionally, garnish the cupcakes with a sprinkle of finely ground Thai tea leaves or a decorative topping of your choice.

4. Serve and Enjoy:

- Serve the Thai Tea Cupcakes immediately, or store them in an airtight container in the refrigerator until ready to serve.
- Enjoy these delicious cupcakes with friends and family, and savor the unique flavors of Thai tea in every bite!

These Thai Tea Cupcakes are a delightful treat, perfect for special occasions, parties, or simply as a sweet indulgence to enjoy any time of the day.

Thai Tea Crème Brûlée

Ingredients:

- 2 cups heavy cream
- 1/2 cup Thai tea leaves
- 6 large egg yolks
- 1/2 cup granulated sugar
- 1 teaspoon vanilla extract
- Granulated sugar, for caramelizing

Instructions:

Preheat your oven to 325°F (160°C). Place 6 ramekins in a large baking dish and set aside.

In a saucepan, heat the heavy cream over medium heat until it begins to simmer. Remove the saucepan from the heat.

Add the Thai tea leaves to the hot cream and let steep for about 10-15 minutes, depending on how strong you want the tea flavor to be. Stir occasionally.

After steeping, strain the cream through a fine-mesh sieve to remove the tea leaves. Press down on the leaves with a spoon to extract as much liquid as possible. Discard the tea leaves.

In a mixing bowl, whisk together the egg yolks and granulated sugar until pale and slightly thickened.

Slowly pour the infused cream into the egg yolk mixture, whisking constantly to prevent curdling.

Stir in the vanilla extract until well combined.

Divide the custard mixture evenly among the prepared ramekins.

Pour hot water into the baking dish, around the ramekins, until it reaches about halfway up the sides of the ramekins. This water bath will help the custards cook gently and evenly.

Carefully transfer the baking dish to the preheated oven and bake for 30-35 minutes, or until the edges are set but the centers still jiggle slightly when shaken.

Remove the baking dish from the oven and let the crème brûlées cool in the water bath for about 15-20 minutes.

Carefully remove the ramekins from the water bath and transfer them to a wire rack to cool completely.

Once cooled, cover the ramekins with plastic wrap and refrigerate for at least 4 hours, or overnight, to chill and set.

Before serving, sprinkle a thin, even layer of granulated sugar over the top of each crème brûlée.

Use a kitchen torch to caramelize the sugar until it forms a golden-brown crust. Alternatively, you can place the ramekins under a broiler for a few minutes until the sugar caramelizes.

Let the crème brûlées sit for a minute to allow the caramelized sugar to harden, then serve immediately and enjoy!

These Thai Tea Crème Brûlées are a delightful fusion of creamy custard and aromatic Thai tea flavors, with a satisfyingly crisp caramelized sugar topping. They make for an elegant and impressive dessert for any occasion.

Thai Tea Mousse

Ingredients:

- 2 cups heavy cream
- 1/2 cup Thai tea leaves
- 1/2 cup granulated sugar
- 1 tablespoon unflavored gelatin
- 2 tablespoons cold water
- 1 teaspoon vanilla extract
- Optional: whipped cream and Thai tea leaves for garnish

Instructions:

In a saucepan, heat the heavy cream over medium heat until it begins to simmer. Remove the saucepan from the heat.
Add the Thai tea leaves to the hot cream and let steep for about 15-20 minutes, stirring occasionally. The longer you steep, the stronger the tea flavor will be.
After steeping, strain the cream through a fine-mesh sieve to remove the tea leaves. Press down on the leaves with a spoon to extract as much liquid as possible. Discard the tea leaves.
In a small bowl, sprinkle the gelatin over the cold water and let it sit for about 5 minutes to soften.
After the gelatin has softened, heat it in the microwave for about 10-15 seconds, or until it has completely dissolved. Be careful not to let it boil.
In a mixing bowl, beat the granulated sugar and vanilla extract into the steeped cream until the sugar is dissolved and the mixture is smooth.
Gradually add the dissolved gelatin to the cream mixture, whisking constantly until well combined.
In a separate mixing bowl, beat the heavy cream until stiff peaks form.
Gently fold the whipped cream into the Thai tea mixture until evenly combined and smooth.
Divide the mousse mixture evenly among serving glasses or ramekins.
Refrigerate the mousse for at least 2-3 hours, or until set.
Before serving, garnish each serving with a dollop of whipped cream and a sprinkle of Thai tea leaves if desired.
Serve the Thai Tea Mousse chilled and enjoy the light and airy texture and aromatic flavors!

This Thai Tea Mousse is a delightful and refreshing dessert that's perfect for any occasion. Its light and fluffy texture combined with the unique flavors of Thai tea make it a delightful treat to enjoy after any meal.

Thai Tea Flan

Ingredients:

For the Caramel:

- 1/2 cup granulated sugar
- 2 tablespoons water

For the Flan:

- 4 large eggs
- 1 can (14 ounces) sweetened condensed milk
- 1 can (12 ounces) evaporated milk
- 1 cup strongly brewed Thai tea, cooled to room temperature and strained
- 1 teaspoon vanilla extract
- Pinch of salt

Instructions:

1. Preheat the Oven:

- Preheat your oven to 350°F (175°C).

2. Prepare the Caramel:

- In a small saucepan, combine the granulated sugar and water over medium heat.
- Stir until the sugar is dissolved, then stop stirring and let it cook.
- Allow the mixture to bubble and caramelize, swirling the pan occasionally to ensure even cooking.
- Once the caramel turns a deep amber color, remove it from the heat and quickly pour it into the bottoms of individual ramekins or a large baking dish. Tilt the dish to spread the caramel evenly across the bottoms. Be careful as the caramel will be extremely hot.

3. Make the Flan Mixture:

- In a mixing bowl, whisk together the eggs, sweetened condensed milk, evaporated milk, cooled Thai tea, vanilla extract, and a pinch of salt until well combined and smooth.

4. Pour the Mixture into Ramekins:

    - Carefully pour the flan mixture over the caramel layer in the ramekins or baking dish.

5. Bake the Flan:

    - Place the ramekins or baking dish into a larger baking pan. Fill the larger pan with hot water until it reaches about halfway up the sides of the ramekins or baking dish. This creates a water bath that helps the flan cook evenly.
    - Carefully transfer the pan to the preheated oven and bake for about 45-50 minutes, or until the flan is set around the edges but still slightly jiggly in the center.
    - Remove the pan from the oven and let the flan cool to room temperature in the water bath.

6. Chill and Serve:

    - Once cooled, carefully remove the ramekins or baking dish from the water bath and refrigerate the flan for at least 4 hours, or preferably overnight, to chill and set completely.

7. Serve the Flan:

    - To serve, run a knife around the edges of each ramekin to loosen the flan. Place a serving plate over the top of each ramekin and quickly flip it over to release the flan onto the plate, allowing the caramel to drizzle over the top.
    - Serve the Thai Tea Flan chilled and enjoy its creamy texture and rich Thai tea flavor!

This Thai Tea Flan is a luxurious and elegant dessert that's perfect for special occasions or any time you want to indulge in a delicious treat with a unique twist.

Thai Tea Cake Roll

Ingredients:

For the Cake:

- 4 large eggs, separated
- 1/2 cup granulated sugar
- 1/4 cup Thai tea, strongly brewed and cooled
- 1/2 cup cake flour
- 1 teaspoon baking powder
- 1/4 teaspoon salt
- 1/4 teaspoon cream of tartar

For the Filling:

- 1 cup heavy cream
- 2 tablespoons powdered sugar
- 1/2 teaspoon vanilla extract

Instructions:

1. Preheat the Oven:

- Preheat your oven to 350°F (175°C). Grease a 10x15-inch jelly roll pan and line it with parchment paper, leaving an overhang on the longer sides. Grease the parchment paper as well.

2. Make the Cake Batter:

- In a mixing bowl, beat the egg yolks with 1/4 cup of granulated sugar until pale and thick. Stir in the brewed Thai tea.
- In a separate bowl, sift together the cake flour, baking powder, and salt. Gradually add the dry ingredients to the egg yolk mixture, stirring until well combined.
- In another clean mixing bowl, beat the egg whites with the cream of tartar until soft peaks form. Gradually add the remaining 1/4 cup of granulated sugar and continue beating until stiff peaks form.

- Gently fold the beaten egg whites into the cake batter until no streaks remain.

3. Bake the Cake:

- Spread the cake batter evenly into the prepared jelly roll pan, smoothing the top with an offset spatula.
- Bake in the preheated oven for 12-15 minutes, or until the cake is lightly golden and springs back when lightly touched.

4. Roll the Cake:

- While the cake is still warm, carefully lift the cake by the parchment paper and invert it onto a clean kitchen towel dusted with powdered sugar.
- Gently peel off the parchment paper from the bottom of the cake.
- Starting from one of the shorter sides, gently roll the cake and the kitchen towel together into a tight spiral. Let the cake cool completely in this rolled-up position.

5. Make the Filling:

- In a mixing bowl, beat the heavy cream with powdered sugar and vanilla extract until stiff peaks form.

6. Assemble the Cake Roll:

- Carefully unroll the cooled cake and kitchen towel.
- Spread the whipped cream filling evenly over the surface of the cake, leaving a small border around the edges.
- Gently roll the cake back up, starting from the same end as before. Use the kitchen towel to help roll the cake.
- Transfer the rolled cake to a serving platter, seam side down.
- Optional: Dust the top of the cake roll with powdered sugar for decoration.

7. Chill and Serve:

- Refrigerate the Thai Tea Cake Roll for at least 1 hour before serving to allow the filling to set.

- Slice and serve the cake roll chilled, and enjoy its light and fluffy texture and delightful Thai tea flavor!

This Thai Tea Cake Roll makes for a beautiful and delicious dessert, perfect for special occasions or as a sweet treat to enjoy any time of the year.

Thai Tea Cookies

Ingredients:

- 2 cups all-purpose flour
- 2 tablespoons finely ground Thai tea leaves
- 1/2 teaspoon baking powder
- 1/4 teaspoon salt
- 1/2 cup unsalted butter, softened
- 3/4 cup granulated sugar
- 1 large egg
- 1 teaspoon vanilla extract

For the Glaze (optional):

- 1 cup powdered sugar
- 2-3 tablespoons strongly brewed Thai tea, cooled

Instructions:

1. Preheat the Oven:

- Preheat your oven to 350°F (175°C). Line baking sheets with parchment paper or silicone baking mats.

2. Prepare the Dry Ingredients:

- In a mixing bowl, whisk together the all-purpose flour, finely ground Thai tea leaves, baking powder, and salt until well combined. Set aside.

3. Cream the Butter and Sugar:

- In a separate mixing bowl, cream together the softened butter and granulated sugar until light and fluffy.

4. Add the Egg and Vanilla:

- Beat in the egg and vanilla extract until smooth and well combined.

5. Combine Wet and Dry Ingredients:

- Gradually add the dry ingredients to the wet ingredients, mixing until a dough forms. Be careful not to overmix.

6. Chill the Dough (Optional):

    - If the dough is too soft to handle, you can cover it and chill it in the refrigerator for about 30 minutes to firm up.

7. Shape the Cookies:

    - Roll the dough into small balls, about 1 inch in diameter, and place them on the prepared baking sheets. Leave some space between the cookies as they will spread slightly during baking.

8. Flatten the Cookies:

    - Use the bottom of a glass or the palm of your hand to gently flatten each cookie ball into a round disk.

9. Bake the Cookies:

    - Bake the cookies in the preheated oven for 10-12 minutes, or until the edges are lightly golden.

10. Cool the Cookies:

    - Allow the cookies to cool on the baking sheets for a few minutes before transferring them to a wire rack to cool completely.

11. Prepare the Glaze (Optional):

    - In a small bowl, whisk together the powdered sugar and brewed Thai tea until smooth and well combined. Adjust the consistency by adding more powdered sugar for a thicker glaze or more Thai tea for a thinner glaze.

12. Glaze the Cookies (Optional):

    - Once the cookies have cooled completely, drizzle or spread the glaze over the top of each cookie using a spoon or pastry brush.

13. Let the Glaze Set:

- Allow the glaze to set completely before serving or storing the cookies.

14. Serve and Enjoy:

- Serve the Thai Tea Cookies as a delightful snack or dessert, and enjoy their aromatic flavor with a cup of Thai tea or your favorite beverage!

These Thai Tea Cookies are perfect for enjoying on their own or for sharing with friends and family during special occasions or gatherings. Enjoy their unique flavor and delicate texture!

Thai Tea Milkshake

Ingredients:

- 1 cup strongly brewed Thai tea, cooled to room temperature
- 2 cups vanilla ice cream
- 1/2 cup milk (adjust to achieve desired consistency)
- 2 tablespoons sweetened condensed milk (optional, for added sweetness)
- Ice cubes (optional, for a colder shake)
- Whipped cream, for topping (optional)
- Thai tea leaves or ground cinnamon, for garnish (optional)

Instructions:

Brew the Thai Tea:
- Brew Thai tea leaves in hot water according to the package instructions to make a strong tea. Let it cool to room temperature.

Prepare the Milkshake:
- In a blender, combine the cooled Thai tea, vanilla ice cream, milk, and sweetened condensed milk (if using).
- Add ice cubes if you prefer a colder milkshake or if you want to achieve a thicker consistency.
- Blend the ingredients until smooth and creamy. Taste and adjust the sweetness or thickness by adding more sweetened condensed milk or milk as needed.

Serve the Milkshake:
- Pour the Thai Tea Milkshake into glasses.
- Optionally, top each milkshake with whipped cream for an extra indulgence.
- Garnish with a sprinkle of Thai tea leaves or ground cinnamon for presentation, if desired.

Enjoy:
- Serve the Thai Tea Milkshake immediately with a straw and enjoy its creamy texture and delightful Thai tea flavor!

This Thai Tea Milkshake is a delightful treat, perfect for cooling down on a hot day or as a sweet indulgence anytime you're craving a refreshing beverage. Adjust the sweetness and thickness to suit your taste preferences, and enjoy this creamy and flavorful milkshake!

Thai Tea Latte

Ingredients:

- 2 cups water
- 2 tablespoons Thai tea leaves
- 2 tablespoons sweetened condensed milk
- 1 cup milk (any type you prefer, such as whole milk, almond milk, or coconut milk)
- Ice cubes (optional, for an iced latte)
- Honey or additional sweetener (optional, to taste)

Instructions:

Brew the Thai Tea:
- In a saucepan, bring 2 cups of water to a boil.
- Once boiling, remove the saucepan from the heat and add the Thai tea leaves.
- Let the tea steep for about 5-7 minutes, or until it reaches your desired strength.
- Strain the brewed tea into a pitcher or container, discarding the tea leaves.

Sweeten the Tea:
- While the tea is still warm, stir in the sweetened condensed milk until it's fully dissolved.
- Taste the tea and adjust the sweetness if needed by adding honey or another sweetener to taste. Keep in mind that the milk will also add sweetness to the latte.

Prepare the Latte:
- If making a hot latte, heat the milk in a separate saucepan or microwave until hot but not boiling.
- Froth the hot milk using a milk frother, whisk, or blender until it becomes frothy and foamy.
- Pour the brewed Thai tea into serving cups, filling each cup about halfway.
- Slowly pour the frothed milk over the tea, using a spoon to hold back the foam if desired.
- If making an iced latte, allow the brewed tea to cool to room temperature or chill it in the refrigerator. Then, pour the chilled tea into a glass filled with ice cubes, leaving room at the top. Top with frothed milk.

Serve and Enjoy:

- Stir the Thai Tea Latte gently to combine the flavors.
- Optionally, garnish with a sprinkle of ground cinnamon or additional sweetened condensed milk drizzle on top.
- Serve the Thai Tea Latte immediately and enjoy the creamy, aromatic flavors!

This homemade Thai Tea Latte is perfect for enjoying as a comforting drink any time of the day. You can customize the sweetness and milk type to suit your preferences. Whether served hot or iced, it's sure to be a delightful treat!

Thai Tea Sorbet

Ingredients:

- 2 cups water
- 2 tablespoons Thai tea leaves
- 1/2 cup granulated sugar (adjust to taste)
- 1/4 cup sweetened condensed milk (optional, for added creaminess)
- 2 tablespoons fresh lime juice (optional, for a tangy twist)
- Lime zest, for garnish (optional)

Instructions:

Brew the Thai Tea:
- In a saucepan, bring 2 cups of water to a boil.
- Once boiling, remove the saucepan from the heat and add the Thai tea leaves.
- Let the tea steep for about 5-7 minutes, or until it reaches your desired strength.
- Strain the brewed tea into a pitcher or container, discarding the tea leaves.

Sweeten the Tea:
- While the tea is still warm, stir in the granulated sugar until it's fully dissolved.
- Taste the tea and adjust the sweetness if needed.

Optional Additions:
- For added creaminess, stir in the sweetened condensed milk until well combined.
- For a tangy twist, add fresh lime juice to the tea mixture and stir to combine. This will give the sorbet a bright and refreshing flavor.

Chill the Mixture:
- Allow the Thai tea mixture to cool to room temperature, then refrigerate it until completely chilled. This usually takes about 2-3 hours.

Freeze the Sorbet:
- Once the mixture is chilled, pour it into an ice cream maker and churn according to the manufacturer's instructions. This typically takes about 20-25 minutes, or until the sorbet reaches a smooth and creamy consistency.
- If you don't have an ice cream maker, you can pour the chilled mixture into a shallow dish and place it in the freezer. Every 30 minutes, use a fork to

scrape and stir the mixture until it's fully frozen and has a sorbet-like texture.

Serve and Garnish:
- Once the sorbet is ready, scoop it into serving bowls or glasses.
- Garnish each serving with a sprinkle of lime zest for added flavor and presentation.
- Serve the Thai Tea Sorbet immediately and enjoy its refreshing taste!

This Thai Tea Sorbet is perfect for serving as a light and refreshing dessert on a hot day. It's bursting with the aromatic flavors of Thai tea and can be customized with additional ingredients to suit your taste preferences. Enjoy this delightful frozen treat!

Thai Tea Granita

Ingredients:

- 4 cups water
- 1/2 cup Thai tea leaves
- 1/2 cup granulated sugar (adjust to taste)
- 1/4 cup sweetened condensed milk (optional, for added creaminess)
- 2 tablespoons fresh lime juice (optional, for a tangy twist)
- Lime zest, for garnish (optional)
- Mint leaves, for garnish (optional)

Instructions:

Brew the Thai Tea:
- In a saucepan, bring 4 cups of water to a boil.
- Once boiling, remove the saucepan from the heat and add the Thai tea leaves.
- Let the tea steep for about 5-7 minutes, or until it reaches your desired strength.
- Strain the brewed tea into a pitcher or container, discarding the tea leaves.

Sweeten the Tea:
- While the tea is still warm, stir in the granulated sugar until it's fully dissolved.
- Taste the tea and adjust the sweetness if needed.

Optional Additions:
- For added creaminess, stir in the sweetened condensed milk until well combined.
- For a tangy twist, add fresh lime juice to the tea mixture and stir to combine. This will give the granita a bright and refreshing flavor.

Chill the Mixture:
- Allow the Thai tea mixture to cool to room temperature, then refrigerate it until completely chilled. This usually takes about 2-3 hours.

Freeze the Granita:
- Once the mixture is chilled, pour it into a shallow baking dish or tray.
- Place the dish in the freezer and let it freeze for about 1 hour.

Scrape and Stir:
- After 1 hour, use a fork to scrape and stir the partially frozen mixture, breaking up any ice crystals that have formed.

- Return the dish to the freezer and continue to freeze for another 1-2 hours, scraping and stirring every 30 minutes, until the granita is fully frozen and has a fluffy, icy texture.

Serve and Garnish:
- Once the granita is ready, use a fork to scrape it into serving bowls or glasses.
- Garnish each serving with a sprinkle of lime zest and mint leaves for added flavor and presentation.
- Serve the Thai Tea Granita immediately and enjoy its refreshing taste!

This Thai Tea Granita is perfect for serving as a light and cooling dessert on a hot day. It's bursting with the aromatic flavors of Thai tea and can be customized with additional ingredients to suit your taste preferences. Enjoy this delightful frozen treat!

Thai Tea Truffles

Ingredients:

- 1 cup heavy cream
- 2 tablespoons Thai tea leaves
- 10 ounces semi-sweet chocolate, finely chopped
- 2 tablespoons unsalted butter, softened
- 1/2 teaspoon vanilla extract
- Cocoa powder, for rolling (optional)
- Finely shredded coconut, for rolling (optional)
- Crushed nuts (such as almonds or pistachios), for rolling (optional)

Instructions:

Infuse the Cream:
- In a saucepan, heat the heavy cream over medium heat until it just begins to simmer.
- Remove the saucepan from the heat and add the Thai tea leaves. Let the mixture steep for about 10-15 minutes to infuse the cream with the Thai tea flavor.
- Strain the infused cream through a fine-mesh sieve or cheesecloth to remove the tea leaves. Press down on the leaves to extract as much liquid as possible. Discard the tea leaves and set the infused cream aside.

Prepare the Chocolate:
- Place the finely chopped semi-sweet chocolate in a heatproof bowl.
- In a small saucepan, heat the infused cream over medium heat until it begins to simmer. Remove from heat.
- Pour the hot cream over the chopped chocolate and let it sit for 1-2 minutes to soften the chocolate.
- Gently stir the mixture with a spatula until the chocolate is completely melted and the mixture is smooth and well combined.
- Stir in the softened butter and vanilla extract until fully incorporated.

Chill the Ganache:
- Cover the bowl with plastic wrap, pressing it directly onto the surface of the chocolate mixture to prevent a skin from forming.
- Refrigerate the ganache for about 2-3 hours, or until firm enough to scoop and roll into truffles.

Shape the Truffles:

- Once the ganache is chilled and firm, use a spoon or a small scoop to portion out small amounts of ganache.
- Roll each portion between your palms to form smooth balls. If the ganache is too soft, you can refrigerate it for a bit longer to firm up.
- Place the rolled truffles on a parchment-lined baking sheet.

Roll and Coat the Truffles (Optional):
- If desired, roll the truffles in cocoa powder, finely shredded coconut, or crushed nuts to coat them.
- Place the coated truffles back on the parchment-lined baking sheet.

Chill the Truffles:
- Once all the truffles are shaped and coated, refrigerate them for about 30 minutes to allow the coatings to set and the truffles to firm up.

Serve and Enjoy:
- Serve the Thai Tea Truffles chilled or at room temperature.
- Store any leftover truffles in an airtight container in the refrigerator for up to 1 week.

These Thai Tea Truffles are rich, creamy, and bursting with the aromatic flavors of Thai tea. They make for an elegant and indulgent treat that's perfect for special occasions or as a homemade gift for chocolate lovers. Enjoy!

Thai Tea Marshmallows

Ingredients:

- 1 cup water
- 2 tablespoons Thai tea leaves
- 3 packets (21 grams) unflavored gelatin
- 1/2 cup cold water
- 1 1/2 cups granulated sugar
- 1 cup light corn syrup
- Pinch of salt
- 1 teaspoon vanilla extract
- Powdered sugar, for dusting

Instructions:

Brew the Thai Tea:
- In a small saucepan, bring 1 cup of water to a boil.
- Remove from heat and add the Thai tea leaves.
- Let the tea steep for about 10-15 minutes to infuse the water with the Thai tea flavor.
- Strain the tea through a fine-mesh sieve or cheesecloth into a measuring cup, pressing down on the leaves to extract as much liquid as possible. Discard the leaves.

Prepare the Gelatin:
- In the bowl of a stand mixer fitted with the whisk attachment, combine the unflavored gelatin and 1/2 cup of cold water. Let it sit for about 10 minutes to bloom.

Make the Sugar Syrup:
- In a medium saucepan, combine the brewed Thai tea, granulated sugar, corn syrup, and a pinch of salt.
- Heat the mixture over medium heat, stirring constantly, until the sugar has completely dissolved.

Cook the Syrup:
- Attach a candy thermometer to the side of the saucepan. Increase the heat to medium-high and bring the mixture to a boil without stirring.
- Continue to cook until the syrup reaches 240°F (115°C), which is the soft ball stage.

Whip the Marshmallow Mixture:
- Once the syrup reaches 240°F (115°C), remove it from the heat.
- With the stand mixer on low speed, slowly pour the hot syrup into the bloomed gelatin.
- Once all the syrup has been added, increase the mixer speed to high and whip the mixture until it becomes thick, white, and fluffy. This usually takes about 8-10 minutes.

Add Flavoring:
- Add the vanilla extract to the marshmallow mixture and continue to whip for another minute to incorporate.

Set the Marshmallows:
- Lightly grease a 9x13-inch baking pan and dust it with powdered sugar.
- Pour the marshmallow mixture into the prepared pan, using a spatula to spread it evenly.
- Dust the top of the marshmallow mixture with additional powdered sugar.
- Let the marshmallows set at room temperature for at least 4 hours, or overnight, until firm and set.

Cut and Coat the Marshmallows:
- Once set, use a sharp knife or cookie cutters to cut the marshmallows into squares or desired shapes.
- Coat the cut edges of the marshmallows with powdered sugar to prevent sticking.

Enjoy:
- Serve the Thai Tea Marshmallows as a sweet treat on their own or use them to top hot chocolate or desserts.
- Store any leftover marshmallows in an airtight container at room temperature for up to 1 week.

These Thai Tea Marshmallows are fluffy, flavorful, and perfect for adding a unique twist to your favorite sweet treats. Enjoy their aromatic Thai tea flavor with every bite!

Thai Tea Soufflé

Ingredients:

- 2 cups whole milk
- 1/2 cup Thai tea leaves
- 4 tablespoons unsalted butter, plus extra for greasing
- 1/4 cup all-purpose flour
- 1/4 cup granulated sugar
- 4 large eggs, separated
- Pinch of salt
- Powdered sugar, for dusting (optional)
- Whipped cream or vanilla ice cream, for serving (optional)

Instructions:

Prepare the Thai Tea Infusion:
- In a saucepan, heat the milk over medium heat until it starts to simmer. Remove from heat.
- Add the Thai tea leaves to the hot milk and let them steep for about 10-15 minutes to infuse the milk with the flavor of the tea.
- Strain the milk through a fine-mesh sieve or cheesecloth to remove the tea leaves. Press down on the leaves to extract as much liquid as possible. Discard the leaves.

Preheat the Oven and Prepare the Ramekins:
- Preheat your oven to 375°F (190°C).
- Grease the inside of 4-6 ramekins with butter. Coat the greased ramekins with granulated sugar, tapping out any excess. This helps the soufflés rise evenly.

Make the Base:
- In a clean saucepan, melt the butter over medium heat. Once melted, add the flour and whisk constantly for about 1-2 minutes to make a roux.
- Gradually pour in the infused milk while whisking continuously to avoid lumps. Cook until the mixture thickens and becomes smooth, about 3-4 minutes.
- Remove the saucepan from the heat and let the mixture cool slightly.

Separate the Eggs:
- Separate the egg yolks from the whites into two separate mixing bowls.

Combine the Ingredients:
- Gradually whisk the egg yolks into the slightly cooled milk mixture until well combined.
- Add a pinch of salt to the egg whites and beat them with an electric mixer until stiff peaks form.

Fold in the Egg Whites:
- Gently fold one-third of the beaten egg whites into the milk mixture to lighten it.
- Carefully fold in the remaining egg whites until just combined. Be gentle to preserve the airiness of the beaten whites.

Bake the Soufflés:
- Divide the soufflé mixture evenly among the prepared ramekins, filling them almost to the top.
- Place the ramekins on a baking sheet and transfer them to the preheated oven.
- Bake for about 15-18 minutes, or until the soufflés have risen and are golden brown on top.

Serve Immediately:
- Remove the soufflés from the oven and dust them with powdered sugar if desired.
- Serve the Thai Tea Soufflés immediately, as they will begin to deflate shortly after being removed from the oven.
- Optionally, serve with a dollop of whipped cream or a scoop of vanilla ice cream on the side for added indulgence.

Enjoy the light and airy texture and aromatic Thai tea flavor of these delightful soufflés!

Thai Tea Crepes

Ingredients:

For the Crepe Batter:

- 1 cup all-purpose flour
- 2 tablespoons Thai tea leaves
- 2 tablespoons granulated sugar
- 1/4 teaspoon salt
- 1 1/2 cups milk
- 3 large eggs
- 2 tablespoons unsalted butter, melted
- 1 teaspoon vanilla extract

For Filling and Topping (Optional):

- Sweetened condensed milk
- Fresh fruit (such as sliced strawberries, bananas, or mangoes)
- Whipped cream
- Toasted coconut flakes

Instructions:

Infuse the Milk:
- In a saucepan, heat the milk over medium heat until it starts to simmer.
- Remove from heat and add the Thai tea leaves. Let steep for about 10-15 minutes to infuse the milk with the flavor of the tea.
- Strain the milk through a fine-mesh sieve or cheesecloth to remove the tea leaves. Press down on the leaves to extract as much liquid as possible. Discard the leaves.

Make the Crepe Batter:
- In a large mixing bowl, whisk together the flour, granulated sugar, and salt.
- Gradually whisk in the infused milk until smooth.
- Add the eggs, melted butter, and vanilla extract, and whisk until well combined and the batter is smooth. Let the batter rest for about 10-15 minutes to allow the flavors to meld.

Cook the Crepes:
- Heat a non-stick skillet or crepe pan over medium heat and lightly grease with butter or cooking spray.
- Pour about 1/4 cup of batter into the center of the skillet and swirl it around to coat the bottom evenly.
- Cook the crepe for about 1-2 minutes, or until the edges start to lift and the bottom is lightly golden.
- Carefully flip the crepe using a spatula and cook for an additional 1-2 minutes on the other side.
- Transfer the cooked crepe to a plate and cover with a clean kitchen towel to keep warm. Repeat with the remaining batter, greasing the skillet as needed.

Assemble the Crepes:
- Once all the crepes are cooked, fill each crepe with your desired filling. Drizzle with sweetened condensed milk, add sliced fruit, and top with whipped cream and toasted coconut flakes if desired.
- Fold the crepes into quarters or roll them up.

Serve and Enjoy:
- Serve the Thai Tea Crepes warm and enjoy their delicious flavor and aroma!

These Thai Tea Crepes are perfect for breakfast, brunch, or dessert. They can be customized with a variety of fillings and toppings to suit your taste preferences. Enjoy this delightful and unique twist on traditional crepes!

Thai Tea Bread Pudding

Ingredients:

- 6 cups stale bread cubes (French bread or brioche works well)
- 2 cups whole milk
- 1/2 cup Thai tea leaves
- 4 large eggs
- 1/2 cup granulated sugar
- 1 teaspoon vanilla extract
- 1/4 teaspoon ground cinnamon
- 1/4 teaspoon ground cardamom (optional)
- Pinch of salt
- 1/2 cup raisins or chopped dried fruits (optional)
- Butter or cooking spray, for greasing the baking dish
- Sweetened condensed milk or caramel sauce, for serving (optional)

Instructions:

Preheat the Oven and Prepare the Bread:
- Preheat your oven to 350°F (175°C).
- Grease a 9x13-inch baking dish with butter or cooking spray.
- Arrange the stale bread cubes in the prepared baking dish in an even layer.

Infuse the Milk:
- In a saucepan, heat the whole milk over medium heat until it just starts to simmer.
- Remove the saucepan from the heat and add the Thai tea leaves.
- Let the mixture steep for about 10-15 minutes to infuse the milk with the flavor of the tea.
- Strain the infused milk through a fine-mesh sieve or cheesecloth to remove the tea leaves. Press down on the leaves to extract as much liquid as possible. Discard the leaves.

Prepare the Custard Mixture:
- In a mixing bowl, whisk together the eggs, granulated sugar, vanilla extract, ground cinnamon, ground cardamom (if using), and a pinch of salt until well combined.
- Gradually whisk in the infused milk until smooth and evenly combined.

Assemble the Bread Pudding:

- Sprinkle the raisins or chopped dried fruits (if using) evenly over the bread cubes in the baking dish.
- Pour the custard mixture over the bread cubes, ensuring that all the bread is soaked in the mixture.
- Gently press down on the bread cubes to help them absorb the custard.

Bake the Bread Pudding:
- Place the baking dish in the preheated oven and bake for 35-40 minutes, or until the bread pudding is set and the top is golden brown.
- The pudding is done when a knife inserted into the center comes out clean.

Serve Warm:
- Remove the bread pudding from the oven and let it cool slightly.
- Serve the Thai Tea Bread Pudding warm, drizzled with sweetened condensed milk or caramel sauce if desired.

Enjoy the comforting and aromatic flavors of this Thai Tea Bread Pudding as a delightful dessert or indulgent breakfast treat!

Thai Tea Tapioca Pudding

Ingredients:

- 1/2 cup small pearl tapioca
- 2 cups water
- 2 cups whole milk
- 1/2 cup Thai tea leaves
- 1/2 cup granulated sugar (adjust to taste)
- 1/4 teaspoon salt
- 1/2 cup coconut milk
- Sweetened condensed milk or coconut cream, for serving (optional)
- Sliced fresh fruit (such as mango or strawberries), for garnish (optional)

Instructions:

Soak the Tapioca:
- Place the small pearl tapioca in a bowl and cover it with cold water. Let it soak for at least 30 minutes, or according to the package instructions.

Brew the Thai Tea:
- In a saucepan, bring 2 cups of water to a boil.
- Remove the saucepan from the heat and add the Thai tea leaves.
- Let the tea steep for about 10-15 minutes to infuse the water with the flavor of the tea.
- Strain the brewed tea through a fine-mesh sieve or cheesecloth to remove the tea leaves. Press down on the leaves to extract as much liquid as possible. Discard the leaves.

Cook the Tapioca:
- In a separate saucepan, combine the soaked tapioca pearls, brewed Thai tea, whole milk, granulated sugar, and salt.
- Bring the mixture to a simmer over medium heat, stirring frequently to prevent the tapioca from sticking to the bottom of the pan.
- Reduce the heat to low and let the mixture simmer gently for about 15-20 minutes, or until the tapioca pearls are translucent and tender, and the mixture has thickened to a pudding-like consistency.
- Stir in the coconut milk and cook for an additional 5 minutes, stirring constantly.

Serve the Tapioca Pudding:

- Remove the tapioca pudding from the heat and let it cool slightly.
- Serve the Thai Tea Tapioca Pudding warm or chilled, topped with a drizzle of sweetened condensed milk or coconut cream if desired.
- Garnish with sliced fresh fruit, such as mango or strawberries, for added flavor and presentation.

Enjoy the creamy texture and aromatic flavors of this Thai Tea Tapioca Pudding as a delightful dessert or comforting snack!

Thai Tea Rice Krispie Treats

Ingredients:

- 4 tablespoons unsalted butter
- 1/2 cup Thai tea leaves
- 10 cups mini marshmallows or 1 package (10 ounces) regular marshmallows
- 6 cups crispy rice cereal (such as Rice Krispies)
- Optional: 1/4 teaspoon vanilla extract
- Optional: Pinch of salt

Instructions:

Infuse the Butter:
- In a saucepan, melt the unsalted butter over low heat.
- Add the Thai tea leaves to the melted butter and stir to combine.
- Let the mixture steep for about 10-15 minutes to infuse the butter with the flavor of the tea.
- Strain the infused butter through a fine-mesh sieve or cheesecloth to remove the tea leaves. Press down on the leaves to extract as much liquid as possible. Discard the leaves.

Prepare the Marshmallow Mixture:
- Return the infused butter to the saucepan over low heat.
- Add the mini marshmallows to the saucepan and stir continuously until they are completely melted and smooth.
- Optional: Stir in the vanilla extract and a pinch of salt for added flavor.

Combine with Crispy Rice Cereal:
- Remove the saucepan from the heat and quickly add the crispy rice cereal to the melted marshmallow mixture.
- Stir until the cereal is evenly coated with the marshmallow mixture.

Form and Press into a Pan:
- Lightly grease a 9x13-inch baking dish with butter or cooking spray.
- Transfer the marshmallow-cereal mixture into the prepared baking dish.
- Use a spatula or wax paper to press the mixture evenly into the pan.

Let Cool and Set:
- Allow the Thai Tea Rice Krispie Treats to cool and set at room temperature for at least 30 minutes, or until firm.
- Once set, cut into squares or rectangles using a sharp knife.

Serve and Enjoy:
- Serve the Thai Tea Rice Krispie Treats as a delightful snack or dessert.
- Store any leftover treats in an airtight container at room temperature for up to several days.

These Thai Tea Rice Krispie Treats are sure to be a hit with their unique flavor and chewy texture. Enjoy them as a tasty treat for any occasion!

Thai Tea Coconut Rice

Ingredients:

- 2 cups jasmine rice
- 2 cups water
- 1 cup Thai tea (brewed strong, using Thai tea leaves and hot water)
- 1 cup coconut milk
- 2 tablespoons granulated sugar (adjust to taste)
- 1/2 teaspoon salt
- Optional: Toasted coconut flakes, for garnish
- Optional: Fresh cilantro or mint leaves, for garnish

Instructions:

Prepare the Thai Tea:
- Brew the Thai tea by steeping Thai tea leaves in hot water for about 5-7 minutes, or according to package instructions. Strain the brewed tea to remove the tea leaves and set it aside.

Rinse the Rice:
- Rinse the jasmine rice under cold water until the water runs clear. This helps remove excess starch and prevents the rice from becoming too sticky when cooked.

Cook the Rice:
- In a rice cooker or a medium saucepan, combine the rinsed jasmine rice, water, brewed Thai tea, coconut milk, granulated sugar, and salt.
- If using a rice cooker, follow the manufacturer's instructions for cooking jasmine rice.
- If cooking on the stovetop, bring the mixture to a boil over medium-high heat. Once boiling, reduce the heat to low, cover, and simmer for about 15-20 minutes, or until the rice is tender and all the liquid has been absorbed.

Fluff and Serve:
- Once the rice is cooked, fluff it gently with a fork to separate the grains.
- Transfer the Thai Tea Coconut Rice to a serving dish.
- Garnish with toasted coconut flakes and fresh cilantro or mint leaves, if desired.

Serve and Enjoy:

- Serve the Thai Tea Coconut Rice as a flavorful side dish or accompaniment to your favorite Thai dishes.
- Enjoy the aromatic flavors of Thai tea and coconut in every bite!

This Thai Tea Coconut Rice is perfect for adding a touch of sweetness and fragrance to your meal. It pairs wonderfully with a variety of Thai-inspired dishes or can be enjoyed on its own as a comforting and flavorful side dish.

Thai Tea Chia Pudding

Ingredients:

- 1/2 cup Thai tea leaves
- 2 cups water
- 1/2 cup chia seeds
- 2 cups coconut milk (or any milk of your choice)
- 2-4 tablespoons honey or sweetener of your choice (adjust to taste)
- Optional toppings: sliced mango, shredded coconut, chopped nuts, or fresh berries

Instructions:

Brew the Thai Tea:
- In a saucepan, bring 2 cups of water to a boil.
- Remove from heat and add the Thai tea leaves.
- Let the tea steep for about 10-15 minutes to infuse the water with the flavor of the tea.
- Strain the brewed tea through a fine-mesh sieve or cheesecloth to remove the tea leaves. Press down on the leaves to extract as much liquid as possible. Discard the leaves.

Mix the Chia Pudding Base:
- In a mixing bowl, combine the brewed Thai tea, chia seeds, coconut milk, and honey or sweetener of your choice. Stir well to combine all the ingredients evenly.

Let it Set:
- Cover the mixing bowl and refrigerate the chia pudding mixture for at least 2 hours, or preferably overnight. This allows the chia seeds to absorb the liquid and create a pudding-like consistency.

Serve and Enjoy:
- Once the chia pudding has set, give it a good stir to redistribute the chia seeds.
- Divide the pudding into serving bowls or jars.
- Top each serving with your favorite toppings, such as sliced mango, shredded coconut, chopped nuts, or fresh berries.
- Serve the Thai Tea Chia Pudding chilled and enjoy it as a delicious and nutritious dessert or breakfast option!

This Thai Tea Chia Pudding is not only flavorful but also packed with fiber, protein, and healthy fats from the chia seeds and coconut milk. It's a versatile dish that you can customize with your favorite toppings and enjoy any time of day.

Thai Tea Pound Cake

Ingredients:

- 1 cup unsalted butter, softened
- 2 cups granulated sugar
- 4 large eggs, at room temperature
- 2 1/2 cups all-purpose flour
- 2 teaspoons baking powder
- 1/2 teaspoon salt
- 1/2 cup brewed Thai tea, cooled to room temperature
- 1/4 cup whole milk
- 1 teaspoon vanilla extract
- Optional: Thai Tea Glaze (see below)

Instructions:

Preheat the Oven and Prepare the Pan:
- Preheat your oven to 350°F (175°C).
- Grease and flour a 9x5-inch loaf pan, or line it with parchment paper for easy removal.

Cream the Butter and Sugar:
- In a large mixing bowl, cream together the softened butter and granulated sugar until light and fluffy, using a hand mixer or stand mixer.

Add the Eggs:
- Add the eggs, one at a time, beating well after each addition until fully incorporated.

Combine Dry Ingredients:
- In a separate bowl, sift together the all-purpose flour, baking powder, and salt.

Mix Wet Ingredients:
- In another bowl, mix the brewed Thai tea, whole milk, and vanilla extract until well combined.

Alternate Adding Dry and Wet Ingredients:
- Gradually add the dry ingredients to the creamed butter and sugar mixture, mixing on low speed until just combined.
- Then, gradually add the wet ingredients, mixing on low speed until the batter is smooth and well combined. Be careful not to overmix.

Bake the Cake:
- Pour the batter into the prepared loaf pan and smooth the top with a spatula.
- Bake in the preheated oven for 50-60 minutes, or until a toothpick inserted into the center of the cake comes out clean.

Cool and Glaze (Optional):
- Allow the cake to cool in the pan for about 10 minutes, then transfer it to a wire rack to cool completely.
- If desired, drizzle the cooled cake with Thai Tea Glaze (see below) for extra flavor and decoration.

Serve and Enjoy:
- Slice the Thai Tea Pound Cake and serve it as a delicious dessert or snack. Enjoy its rich and aromatic flavors!

Optional Thai Tea Glaze:

Ingredients:

- 1 cup powdered sugar
- 2-3 tablespoons brewed Thai tea, cooled to room temperature

Instructions:

In a small bowl, whisk together the powdered sugar and brewed Thai tea until smooth and well combined.
Drizzle the glaze over the cooled pound cake using a spoon or piping bag.
Allow the glaze to set for a few minutes before slicing and serving the cake.

This Thai Tea Pound Cake is sure to impress with its unique flavors and tender crumb.

Enjoy it with a cup of Thai tea for a delightful treat!

Thai Tea Scones

Ingredients:

- 2 cups all-purpose flour
- 1/4 cup granulated sugar
- 1 tablespoon baking powder
- 1/2 teaspoon salt
- 1/2 cup unsalted butter, cold and cut into small pieces
- 2 tablespoons Thai tea leaves
- 1/2 cup milk or heavy cream
- 1 large egg
- 1 teaspoon vanilla extract
- Optional: Thai Tea Glaze (see below)

Instructions:

Preheat the Oven and Prepare Baking Sheet:
- Preheat your oven to 400°F (200°C).
- Line a baking sheet with parchment paper or lightly grease it.

Prepare the Thai Tea:
- In a small saucepan, heat the milk or heavy cream until it starts to simmer.
- Remove from heat and add the Thai tea leaves.
- Let the tea steep for about 10-15 minutes to infuse the milk or cream with the flavor of the tea.
- Strain the infused milk or cream through a fine-mesh sieve or cheesecloth to remove the tea leaves. Press down on the leaves to extract as much liquid as possible. Discard the leaves.

Make the Dough:
- In a large mixing bowl, whisk together the flour, granulated sugar, baking powder, and salt.
- Cut in the cold butter pieces using a pastry cutter or fork until the mixture resembles coarse crumbs.
- In a separate bowl, whisk together the infused milk or cream, egg, and vanilla extract until well combined.
- Pour the wet ingredients into the dry ingredients and stir until just combined. Be careful not to overmix.

Shape and Cut the Scones:

- Transfer the dough onto a lightly floured surface and gently knead it a few times until it comes together.
- Pat the dough into a circle or rectangle about 1 inch thick.
- Use a sharp knife or a pastry cutter to cut the dough into 8 triangular wedges or your desired shape.

Bake the Scones:
- Place the shaped scones onto the prepared baking sheet, leaving some space between each scone.
- Bake in the preheated oven for 15-18 minutes, or until the scones are lightly golden brown on top and cooked through.

Optional Thai Tea Glaze:
- Allow the scones to cool slightly before drizzling them with Thai Tea Glaze (see below) for extra flavor and decoration.

Serve and Enjoy:
- Serve the Thai Tea Scones warm or at room temperature, paired with your favorite spread or enjoyed on their own.

Optional Thai Tea Glaze:

Ingredients:

- 1 cup powdered sugar
- 2-3 tablespoons brewed Thai tea, cooled to room temperature

Instructions:

In a small bowl, whisk together the powdered sugar and brewed Thai tea until smooth and well combined.
Drizzle the glaze over the cooled scones using a spoon or piping bag.
Allow the glaze to set for a few minutes before serving the scones.

These Thai Tea Scones are perfect for breakfast, brunch, or afternoon tea. Enjoy their unique flavor and tender texture with every bite!

Thai Tea Parfait

Ingredients:

- 1 cup brewed Thai tea, cooled to room temperature
- 2 cups Greek yogurt (plain or vanilla flavored)
- 2-3 tablespoons honey or sweetener of your choice, to taste
- 1 cup granola
- 1 cup mixed fresh fruit (such as mango, pineapple, and strawberries), diced
- Optional toppings: shredded coconut, chopped nuts, or Thai tea syrup

Instructions:

Prepare the Thai Tea Yogurt:
- In a mixing bowl, combine the brewed Thai tea with Greek yogurt and honey or sweetener. Stir well until smooth and fully incorporated. Adjust sweetness to your taste preference.

Assemble the Parfaits:
- In serving glasses or bowls, layer the ingredients in the following order:
    - A spoonful of Thai tea yogurt mixture
    - A layer of granola
    - A layer of mixed fresh fruit
    - Repeat the layers until the glasses are filled, ending with a final layer of Thai tea yogurt on top.

Add Optional Toppings:
- Garnish the top of each parfait with shredded coconut, chopped nuts, or a drizzle of Thai tea syrup for extra flavor and decoration.

Serve and Enjoy:
- Serve the Thai Tea Parfaits immediately as a refreshing dessert or snack.
- Enjoy the creamy texture, crunchy granola, and vibrant flavors of fresh fruit with every spoonful!

Optional Thai Tea Syrup:

Ingredients:

- 1/2 cup brewed Thai tea
- 1/2 cup granulated sugar

Instructions:

In a small saucepan, combine the brewed Thai tea and granulated sugar. Heat the mixture over medium heat, stirring constantly, until the sugar has dissolved and the mixture has thickened slightly.
Remove from heat and let the syrup cool completely before using.
Drizzle the cooled syrup over the Thai Tea Parfaits for added sweetness and flavor.

Enjoy this Thai Tea Parfait as a delightful and refreshing dessert, perfect for any occasion!

Thai Tea Ice Pops

Ingredients:

- 2 cups brewed Thai tea, cooled to room temperature
- 1 cup coconut milk
- 2-4 tablespoons honey or sweetener of your choice, to taste
- Optional: Sliced fresh fruit (such as mango or strawberries), for added texture and flavor

Instructions:

Prepare the Thai Tea Mixture:
- In a mixing bowl, combine the brewed Thai tea with coconut milk and honey or sweetener. Stir well until fully incorporated. Adjust sweetness to your taste preference.

Add Optional Fresh Fruit:
- If desired, add sliced fresh fruit, such as mango or strawberries, to the Thai tea mixture. This will add texture and extra flavor to the ice pops.

Fill Ice Pop Molds:
- Pour the Thai tea mixture into ice pop molds, leaving a little space at the top for expansion.
- If using fresh fruit, make sure to distribute it evenly among the molds.

Insert Sticks:
- Place ice pop sticks or handles into each mold, ensuring they are centered and upright.

Freeze:
- Transfer the filled ice pop molds to the freezer and let them freeze for at least 4-6 hours, or until completely frozen solid.

Unmold and Serve:
- Once the ice pops are frozen, remove them from the molds by running warm water over the outside of the molds for a few seconds. This will help release the ice pops easily.
- Serve the Thai Tea Ice Pops immediately and enjoy their refreshing flavor!

Feel free to customize these ice pops with your favorite fruits or additional ingredients for a unique twist. Enjoy this delicious and cooling treat on a hot day!

Thai Tea Popsicles

Ingredients:

- 2 cups brewed Thai tea, cooled to room temperature
- 1 cup coconut milk
- 2-4 tablespoons honey or sweetener of your choice, to taste
- Optional: Sliced fresh fruit (such as mango or strawberries), for added texture and flavor

Instructions:

Prepare the Thai Tea Mixture:
- In a mixing bowl, combine the brewed Thai tea with coconut milk and honey or sweetener. Stir well until fully incorporated. Adjust sweetness to your taste preference.

Add Optional Fresh Fruit:
- If desired, add sliced fresh fruit, such as mango or strawberries, to the Thai tea mixture. This will add texture and extra flavor to the popsicles.

Fill Popsicle Molds:
- Pour the Thai tea mixture into popsicle molds, leaving a little space at the top for expansion.
- If using fresh fruit, make sure to distribute it evenly among the molds.

Insert Sticks:
- Place popsicle sticks or handles into each mold, ensuring they are centered and upright.

Freeze:
- Transfer the filled popsicle molds to the freezer and let them freeze for at least 4-6 hours, or until completely frozen solid.

Unmold and Serve:
- Once the popsicles are frozen, remove them from the molds by running warm water over the outside of the molds for a few seconds. This will help release the popsicles easily.
- Serve the Thai Tea Popsicles immediately and enjoy their refreshing flavor!

These Thai Tea Popsicles are perfect for cooling off on a hot day and can be enjoyed as a delicious and refreshing treat. Feel free to experiment with different flavors or add-ins to customize them to your liking. Enjoy!

Thai Tea Smoothie

Ingredients:

- 1 cup brewed Thai tea, cooled to room temperature
- 1/2 cup coconut milk
- 1 ripe banana, frozen
- 1/2 cup ice cubes
- 1 tablespoon honey or sweetener of your choice, to taste
- Optional: 1/4 teaspoon vanilla extract or ground cinnamon for added flavor

Instructions:

Brew Thai Tea:
- Brew Thai tea according to package instructions and let it cool to room temperature.

Prepare Ingredients:
- Peel and slice a ripe banana, then freeze the slices for at least 2 hours or overnight.

Blend Ingredients:
- In a blender, combine the cooled Thai tea, coconut milk, frozen banana slices, ice cubes, honey, and any optional flavorings, such as vanilla extract or ground cinnamon.
- Blend on high speed until smooth and creamy, scraping down the sides of the blender as needed.

Taste and Adjust:
- Taste the smoothie and adjust the sweetness or flavorings if necessary. Add more honey or flavorings to suit your taste preference.

Serve:
- Pour the Thai Tea Smoothie into glasses and serve immediately.
- Optionally, garnish with a sprinkle of ground cinnamon or a drizzle of honey on top for extra flavor and decoration.

Enjoy:
- Enjoy the refreshing and creamy Thai Tea Smoothie as a delicious breakfast drink, snack, or dessert.

Feel free to customize this smoothie recipe by adding other ingredients such as mango, pineapple, or spinach for extra nutrients and flavor. Experiment with different variations to create your perfect Thai Tea Smoothie!

Thai Tea Jelly

Ingredients:

- 2 cups brewed Thai tea, cooled to room temperature
- 1/2 cup sugar
- 1/4 cup water
- 2 tablespoons unflavored gelatin powder
- 1/4 cup sweetened condensed milk (optional, for added sweetness and creaminess)

Instructions:

Prepare Thai Tea Mixture:
- In a saucepan, combine the brewed Thai tea and sugar. Stir until the sugar is dissolved.

Bloom Gelatin:
- In a small bowl, sprinkle the gelatin powder over 1/4 cup of water. Let it sit for about 5 minutes to bloom.

Heat Thai Tea Mixture:
- Place the saucepan with the Thai tea mixture over medium heat. Heat until it is hot but not boiling.

Dissolve Gelatin:
- Add the bloomed gelatin mixture to the hot Thai tea mixture. Stir until the gelatin is completely dissolved.

Optional: Add Sweetened Condensed Milk:
- If using sweetened condensed milk, stir it into the Thai tea mixture until well combined. This will add sweetness and creaminess to the jelly.

Pour Into Molds:
- Pour the Thai tea mixture into molds of your choice. You can use individual serving cups, silicone molds, or an ice cube tray.

Chill:
- Place the molds in the refrigerator and let the jelly set for at least 4 hours, or until firm.

Serve:
- Once the jelly is set, remove it from the molds and serve chilled.

Optional: Garnish:
- Garnish the Thai Tea Jelly with a drizzle of sweetened condensed milk or a sprinkle of crushed ice for added presentation.

Enjoy the Thai Tea Jelly as a refreshing dessert on its own, or serve it with fresh fruit, whipped cream, or a scoop of ice cream for an extra special treat!

Thai Tea Custard Tart

Ingredients:

For the Crust:

- 1 1/2 cups all-purpose flour
- 1/2 cup unsalted butter, cold and cubed
- 1/4 cup granulated sugar
- 1 egg yolk
- 1-2 tablespoons cold water, if needed

For the Filling:

- 1 1/2 cups brewed Thai tea, cooled to room temperature
- 1 cup heavy cream
- 1/2 cup granulated sugar
- 4 large eggs
- 1 teaspoon vanilla extract
- Pinch of salt

Instructions:

Prepare the Crust:
- In a food processor, combine the flour and cubed butter. Pulse until the mixture resembles coarse crumbs.
- Add the sugar and egg yolk, and pulse again until the dough starts to come together. If the dough is too dry, add cold water, one tablespoon at a time, until it forms a ball.
- Flatten the dough into a disk, wrap it in plastic wrap, and refrigerate for at least 30 minutes.

Preheat the Oven:
- Preheat your oven to 375°F (190°C).

Roll Out the Dough:
- On a lightly floured surface, roll out the chilled dough into a circle large enough to fit your tart pan. Transfer the dough to the tart pan and press it gently into the bottom and sides. Trim any excess dough.

Blind Bake the Crust:

- Line the tart crust with parchment paper and fill it with pie weights or dried beans.
- Bake in the preheated oven for 15 minutes. Remove the parchment paper and weights, and bake for an additional 5 minutes, or until the crust is golden brown. Remove from the oven and let it cool slightly.

Prepare the Filling:
- In a mixing bowl, whisk together the brewed Thai tea, heavy cream, sugar, eggs, vanilla extract, and salt until well combined.

Bake the Tart:
- Pour the custard filling into the pre-baked tart crust.
- Place the tart pan on a baking sheet and transfer it to the oven.
- Bake for 30-35 minutes, or until the custard is set and the edges are golden brown.

Cool and Serve:
- Allow the Thai Tea Custard Tart to cool completely before slicing and serving.
- Optionally, garnish with whipped cream or a sprinkle of powdered sugar before serving.

Enjoy this Thai Tea Custard Tart as a delicious and unique dessert, perfect for any occasion!

Thai Tea Rice Balls

Ingredients:

- 1 cup glutinous rice flour
- 1/4 cup Thai tea leaves
- 1/4 cup granulated sugar
- Water, as needed
- Shredded coconut (optional, for coating)
- Sesame seeds (optional, for garnish)

Instructions:

Prepare Thai Tea Infusion:
- In a heatproof bowl, steep the Thai tea leaves in hot water for about 10-15 minutes to make a concentrated tea infusion. Strain the tea leaves and discard them. You should have about 1/2 cup of Thai tea infusion.

Make the Rice Dough:
- In a mixing bowl, combine the glutinous rice flour and granulated sugar.
- Gradually add the Thai tea infusion to the rice flour mixture while stirring continuously until a smooth dough forms. If the dough is too dry, add a little more water, one tablespoon at a time, until it comes together.

Form Rice Balls:
- Take small portions of the rice dough and roll them into small balls, about 1 inch in diameter. If desired, you can also flatten the balls slightly to form discs.

Optional Coating:
- If using shredded coconut, roll the rice balls in the shredded coconut until evenly coated. This will add texture and flavor to the rice balls.

Cook the Rice Balls:
- Bring a pot of water to a boil over medium heat.
- Carefully drop the rice balls into the boiling water. Cook them for about 2-3 minutes, or until they float to the surface and are cooked through. Be careful not to overcrowd the pot.

Serve:
- Once cooked, remove the rice balls from the boiling water using a slotted spoon and transfer them to a bowl of cold water to cool briefly.

- Drain the rice balls and place them on a serving plate. If desired, sprinkle sesame seeds over the rice balls for garnish.

Enjoy:
- Serve the Thai Tea Rice Balls as a delicious dessert or snack. They can be enjoyed warm or chilled.

These Thai Tea Rice Balls are a delightful treat with the unique flavor of Thai tea. They make a perfect addition to any dessert spread or afternoon snack. Enjoy!

Thai Tea Shortbread

Ingredients:

- 1 cup unsalted butter, softened
- 1/2 cup powdered sugar
- 2 tablespoons Thai tea leaves
- 2 cups all-purpose flour
- 1/4 teaspoon salt
- Additional powdered sugar, for dusting (optional)

Instructions:

Prepare Thai Tea Infusion:
- In a small saucepan, heat the butter over low heat until melted. Add the Thai tea leaves and let them steep in the melted butter for about 15-20 minutes. Remove from heat and let the mixture cool to room temperature. Strain the butter to remove the tea leaves, pressing down to extract all the flavor.

Cream Butter and Sugar:
- In a mixing bowl, cream together the softened butter and powdered sugar until light and fluffy.

Add Thai Tea Butter:
- Gradually add the cooled Thai tea-infused butter to the creamed mixture, beating until well combined.

Mix Dry Ingredients:
- In a separate bowl, whisk together the all-purpose flour and salt.

Combine Wet and Dry Ingredients:
- Gradually add the flour mixture to the butter mixture, mixing until a dough forms. Be careful not to overmix.

Chill Dough:
- Shape the dough into a disk, wrap it in plastic wrap, and refrigerate for at least 30 minutes to firm up.

Preheat Oven:
- Preheat your oven to 350°F (175°C) and line a baking sheet with parchment paper.

Roll Out Dough:
- On a lightly floured surface, roll out the chilled dough to about 1/4 inch thickness.

Cut Out Cookies:
- Use cookie cutters to cut out shapes from the dough. Place the cookies onto the prepared baking sheet, leaving some space between each cookie.

Bake:
- Bake the cookies in the preheated oven for 12-15 minutes, or until the edges are lightly golden brown.

Cool and Serve:
- Allow the cookies to cool on the baking sheet for a few minutes before transferring them to a wire rack to cool completely. Optionally, dust the cooled cookies with powdered sugar before serving.

Enjoy:
- Enjoy your Thai Tea Shortbread cookies with a cup of Thai tea or your favorite hot beverage!

These Thai Tea Shortbread cookies are buttery, fragrant, and perfect for enjoying as a snack or dessert. They also make lovely gifts for friends and family!

Thai Tea Waffles

Ingredients:

- 2 cups all-purpose flour
- 2 tablespoons Thai tea leaves
- 2 teaspoons baking powder
- 1/4 teaspoon baking soda
- 1/4 teaspoon salt
- 2 tablespoons granulated sugar
- 2 large eggs, separated
- 1 1/2 cups buttermilk
- 1/2 cup unsalted butter, melted
- 1 teaspoon vanilla extract
- Cooking spray or additional melted butter, for greasing the waffle iron

Instructions:

Prepare Thai Tea Infusion:
- In a small saucepan, heat the buttermilk over low heat until it starts to steam. Add the Thai tea leaves and let them steep in the hot buttermilk for about 10-15 minutes. Strain the milk to remove the tea leaves, pressing down to extract all the flavor. Allow the infused buttermilk to cool to room temperature.

Preheat Waffle Iron:
- Preheat your waffle iron according to the manufacturer's instructions.

Mix Dry Ingredients:
- In a large mixing bowl, whisk together the all-purpose flour, baking powder, baking soda, salt, and granulated sugar.

Mix Wet Ingredients:
- In a separate bowl, whisk together the egg yolks, infused buttermilk, melted butter, and vanilla extract until well combined.

Combine Wet and Dry Ingredients:
- Gradually add the wet ingredients to the dry ingredients, stirring until just combined. Do not overmix; a few lumps are okay.

Beat Egg Whites:
- In another clean mixing bowl, beat the egg whites with a hand mixer or stand mixer until stiff peaks form.

Fold in Egg Whites:

- Gently fold the beaten egg whites into the waffle batter until just incorporated. Be careful not to deflate the egg whites.

Cook Waffles:
- Lightly grease the preheated waffle iron with cooking spray or melted butter.
- Pour an appropriate amount of batter onto the waffle iron according to its size, and cook until the waffles are golden brown and crispy.

Serve:
- Serve the Thai Tea Waffles warm with your favorite toppings, such as fresh fruit, whipped cream, maple syrup, or condensed milk.

Enjoy:
- Enjoy the unique and aromatic flavors of Thai tea infused into these delicious waffles for a delightful breakfast or brunch experience!

These Thai Tea Waffles are sure to impress with their fragrant aroma and distinctive taste. Serve them for a special occasion or whenever you're craving a flavorful twist on classic waffles!

Thai Tea Donuts

Ingredients:

For the donuts:

- 2 cups all-purpose flour
- 1/2 cup granulated sugar
- 2 teaspoons baking powder
- 1/2 teaspoon salt
- 2 tablespoons Thai tea leaves
- 2 large eggs
- 3/4 cup milk
- 1/4 cup unsalted butter, melted
- 1 teaspoon vanilla extract
- Oil for frying

For the glaze:

- 1 cup powdered sugar
- 2-3 tablespoons brewed Thai tea, cooled
- 1/2 teaspoon vanilla extract

Instructions:

Make the Thai Tea Infusion:
- In a small saucepan, heat the milk until it just begins to steam. Add the Thai tea leaves and let them steep for 10-15 minutes. Strain the milk to remove the tea leaves and allow it to cool to room temperature.

Prepare the Donut Batter:
- In a large mixing bowl, whisk together the flour, sugar, baking powder, and salt.
- In another bowl, whisk the eggs, cooled Thai tea-infused milk, melted butter, and vanilla extract until well combined.
- Pour the wet ingredients into the dry ingredients and mix until just combined. Be careful not to overmix.

Fry the Donuts:

- Heat oil in a deep fryer or heavy-bottomed pot to 350°F (175°C).
- Drop spoonfuls of the batter into the hot oil, frying a few at a time to avoid overcrowding. Fry for 2-3 minutes per side, or until golden brown.
- Remove the donuts from the oil using a slotted spoon and place them on a paper towel-lined plate to drain excess oil.

Make the Glaze:
- In a shallow bowl, whisk together the powdered sugar, brewed Thai tea, and vanilla extract until smooth.

Glaze the Donuts:
- Dip each donut into the glaze, coating it evenly. You can dip them once for a light glaze or twice for a thicker coating.
- Place the glazed donuts on a wire rack to allow any excess glaze to drip off.

Serve:
- Serve the Thai Tea Donuts warm and enjoy their unique flavor!

These Thai Tea Donuts are sure to be a hit with their aromatic flavor and soft texture.

They make a delightful treat for breakfast or dessert!

Thai Tea Pancakes

Ingredients:

- 1 cup all-purpose flour
- 2 tablespoons Thai tea leaves
- 2 tablespoons granulated sugar
- 1 teaspoon baking powder
- 1/2 teaspoon baking soda
- 1/4 teaspoon salt
- 1 cup buttermilk
- 1 large egg
- 2 tablespoons unsalted butter, melted
- 1 teaspoon vanilla extract
- Oil or butter for greasing the pan

Optional Toppings:

- Maple syrup
- Whipped cream
- Fresh berries
- Sliced bananas
- Chopped nuts

Instructions:

Prepare Thai Tea Infusion:
- In a small saucepan, heat the buttermilk until it just begins to steam. Add the Thai tea leaves and let them steep for 10-15 minutes. Strain the buttermilk to remove the tea leaves and allow it to cool to room temperature.

Make the Pancake Batter:
- In a large mixing bowl, whisk together the flour, sugar, baking powder, baking soda, and salt.
- In another bowl, whisk the egg, cooled Thai tea-infused buttermilk, melted butter, and vanilla extract until well combined.
- Pour the wet ingredients into the dry ingredients and stir until just combined. Do not overmix; a few lumps are okay.

Cook the Pancakes:

- Heat a non-stick skillet or griddle over medium heat and lightly grease with oil or butter.
- Pour about 1/4 cup of batter onto the skillet for each pancake. Cook until bubbles form on the surface of the pancakes and the edges begin to set, about 2-3 minutes.
- Flip the pancakes and cook for an additional 1-2 minutes, or until golden brown and cooked through.
- Repeat with the remaining batter, adding more oil or butter to the skillet as needed.

Serve:
- Serve the Thai Tea Pancakes warm with your choice of toppings, such as maple syrup, whipped cream, fresh berries, sliced bananas, or chopped nuts.

Enjoy:
- Enjoy these aromatic and flavorful Thai Tea Pancakes for a delicious breakfast or brunch treat!

These Thai Tea Pancakes are sure to impress with their unique flavor and fluffy texture. They're perfect for a special weekend breakfast or any time you're craving something a little different!

Thai Tea Caramel Sauce

Ingredients:

- 1 cup granulated sugar
- 1/4 cup water
- 1 cup heavy cream
- 2 tablespoons Thai tea leaves
- 2 tablespoons unsalted butter
- 1/2 teaspoon vanilla extract
- Pinch of salt

Instructions:

Prepare Thai Tea Infusion:
- In a small saucepan, heat the heavy cream until it just begins to simmer. Add the Thai tea leaves and let them steep for 10-15 minutes. Strain the cream to remove the tea leaves and set aside.

Make the Caramel Sauce:
- In a large, heavy-bottomed saucepan, combine the granulated sugar and water over medium heat. Stir until the sugar is dissolved.

Caramelize the Sugar:
- Once the sugar has dissolved, stop stirring and allow the mixture to come to a boil. Let it boil, swirling the pan occasionally, until it turns a deep amber color, about 5-7 minutes. Be careful not to let it burn.

Add the Cream:
- Carefully pour the steeped cream into the caramelized sugar mixture, stirring constantly. Be cautious as the mixture will bubble up vigorously.

Finish the Sauce:
- Stir in the unsalted butter, vanilla extract, and a pinch of salt. Continue to cook, stirring constantly, until the butter is melted and the sauce is smooth and thickened, about 2-3 minutes.

Cool and Store:
- Remove the saucepan from the heat and let the Thai Tea Caramel Sauce cool slightly before transferring it to a heatproof container or jar.
- Allow the sauce to cool completely before covering and storing it in the refrigerator. It will thicken further as it cools.

Serve:

- Serve the Thai Tea Caramel Sauce drizzled over desserts such as ice cream, cakes, pancakes, or waffles. It adds a delightful Thai tea flavor to your favorite treats.

Enjoy:
- Enjoy the rich and aromatic flavors of this Thai Tea Caramel Sauce as a delicious topping for your favorite desserts!

This Thai Tea Caramel Sauce is sure to impress with its unique flavor profile and versatility. It's perfect for adding a touch of Thai-inspired flair to your dessert creations!

Thai Tea Tres Leches Cake

Ingredients:

For the cake:

- 1 1/2 cups all-purpose flour
- 1 tablespoon Thai tea leaves
- 1 teaspoon baking powder
- 1/2 teaspoon baking soda
- 1/4 teaspoon salt
- 4 large eggs, separated
- 1 cup granulated sugar
- 1/3 cup whole milk
- 1/4 cup unsalted butter, melted
- 1 teaspoon vanilla extract

For the tres leches mixture:

- 1 (14 oz) can sweetened condensed milk
- 1 (12 oz) can evaporated milk
- 1 cup coconut milk
- 1 teaspoon vanilla extract

For the whipped cream topping:

- 1 cup heavy cream
- 2 tablespoons powdered sugar
- 1 teaspoon vanilla extract

Instructions:

Prepare the Thai Tea Infusion:
- In a small saucepan, heat the whole milk until it begins to steam. Add the Thai tea leaves and let them steep for 10-15 minutes. Strain the milk to remove the tea leaves and set aside to cool.

Make the Cake:
- Preheat the oven to 350°F (175°C). Grease and flour a 9x13 inch baking pan.

- In a mixing bowl, sift together the flour, baking powder, baking soda, and salt.
- In another bowl, beat the egg whites until stiff peaks form.
- In a separate large mixing bowl, beat the egg yolks with the sugar until pale and fluffy. Stir in the melted butter and vanilla extract.
- Gradually add the dry ingredients to the egg yolk mixture, alternating with the cooled Thai tea-infused milk, until just combined.
- Gently fold in the beaten egg whites until no streaks remain.
- Pour the batter into the prepared baking pan and smooth the top.
- Bake for 25-30 minutes, or until a toothpick inserted into the center comes out clean.
- Remove the cake from the oven and let it cool in the pan for 10 minutes.

Make the Tres Leches Mixture:
- In a large measuring cup or bowl, whisk together the sweetened condensed milk, evaporated milk, coconut milk, and vanilla extract until well combined.

Soak the Cake:
- Use a fork or skewer to poke holes all over the surface of the warm cake.
- Slowly pour the tres leches mixture over the cake, allowing it to absorb the liquid. Cover the cake and refrigerate for at least 4 hours, or overnight, to allow the flavors to meld and the cake to fully absorb the liquid.

Make the Whipped Cream Topping:
- In a mixing bowl, beat the heavy cream, powdered sugar, and vanilla extract until stiff peaks form.
- Spread the whipped cream over the top of the chilled cake.

Serve:
- Slice the Thai Tea Tres Leches Cake and serve chilled. Enjoy the rich, moist cake with its unique Thai tea flavor and creamy topping!

This Thai Tea Tres Leches Cake is a delightful fusion of flavors and textures, perfect for any occasion. Enjoy its rich and moist texture with a hint of aromatic Thai tea in every bite!

Thai Tea Layer Cake

Ingredients:

For the cake:

- 2 cups all-purpose flour
- 2 tablespoons Thai tea leaves
- 1 tablespoon baking powder
- 1/2 teaspoon baking soda
- 1/4 teaspoon salt
- 1/2 cup unsalted butter, softened
- 1 cup granulated sugar
- 3 large eggs
- 1 teaspoon vanilla extract
- 1 cup buttermilk, at room temperature

For the frosting:

- 1 1/2 cups unsalted butter, softened
- 4 cups powdered sugar
- 2-3 tablespoons brewed Thai tea, cooled
- 1 teaspoon vanilla extract
- Pinch of salt

Instructions:

Prepare the Thai Tea Infusion:
- In a small saucepan, heat the buttermilk until it just begins to steam. Add the Thai tea leaves and let them steep for 10-15 minutes. Strain the buttermilk to remove the tea leaves and set aside to cool.

Make the Cake:
- Preheat the oven to 350°F (175°C). Grease and flour two 9-inch round cake pans.
- In a mixing bowl, sift together the flour, baking powder, baking soda, and salt. Set aside.

- In a large mixing bowl, cream together the softened butter and granulated sugar until light and fluffy.
- Beat in the eggs, one at a time, until well combined. Stir in the vanilla extract.
- Gradually add the dry ingredients to the wet ingredients, alternating with the cooled Thai tea-infused buttermilk, beginning and ending with the dry ingredients. Mix until just combined.
- Divide the batter evenly between the prepared cake pans and smooth the tops with a spatula.
- Bake for 25-30 minutes, or until a toothpick inserted into the center of the cakes comes out clean.
- Remove the cakes from the oven and let them cool in the pans for 10 minutes before transferring them to wire racks to cool completely.

Make the Frosting:

- In a mixing bowl, beat the softened butter until creamy.
- Gradually add the powdered sugar, one cup at a time, beating well after each addition until smooth and fluffy.
- Add the cooled brewed Thai tea, vanilla extract, and a pinch of salt. Beat until well combined and the frosting is smooth and creamy.

Assemble the Cake:

- Place one cake layer on a serving plate or cake stand. Spread a layer of frosting over the top.
- Place the second cake layer on top and spread the remaining frosting over the top and sides of the cake.
- Smooth the frosting with a spatula for an even finish.

Decorate (optional):

- Garnish the top of the cake with additional Thai tea leaves or a sprinkle of powdered sugar for decoration.

Chill and Serve:

- Refrigerate the cake for at least 30 minutes before slicing and serving to allow the frosting to set.
- Slice and serve the Thai Tea Layer Cake and enjoy its delightful flavor and texture!

This Thai Tea Layer Cake is sure to impress with its aromatic Thai tea flavor and creamy frosting. It's perfect for special occasions or as a delightful treat for any tea lover!

Thai Tea Pecan Pie

Ingredients:

For the pie crust:

- 1 1/4 cups all-purpose flour
- 1/2 teaspoon salt
- 1/2 cup unsalted butter, chilled and diced
- 1/4 cup ice water

For the filling:

- 1 cup Thai tea concentrate (brewed Thai tea that has been cooled)
- 3 large eggs
- 1 cup light corn syrup
- 1/2 cup packed brown sugar
- 2 tablespoons unsalted butter, melted
- 1 teaspoon vanilla extract
- 1/4 teaspoon salt
- 1 1/2 cups pecan halves

Instructions:

Prepare the Pie Crust:
- In a food processor, combine the flour and salt. Add the chilled, diced butter and pulse until the mixture resembles coarse crumbs.
- Gradually add the ice water, 1 tablespoon at a time, and pulse until the dough comes together into a ball.
- Flatten the dough into a disk, wrap it in plastic wrap, and refrigerate for at least 1 hour.

Preheat the Oven:
- Preheat your oven to 350°F (175°C).

Roll Out the Pie Crust:
- On a lightly floured surface, roll out the chilled pie dough into a circle large enough to fit into a 9-inch pie dish. Transfer the dough to the pie dish and trim any excess overhang. Crimp the edges as desired.

Prepare the Filling:
- In a mixing bowl, whisk together the Thai tea concentrate, eggs, corn syrup, brown sugar, melted butter, vanilla extract, and salt until well combined.

Assemble the Pie:
- Scatter the pecan halves evenly over the bottom of the prepared pie crust.
- Pour the filling mixture over the pecans, making sure they are evenly coated.

Bake the Pie:
- Place the pie in the preheated oven and bake for 50-60 minutes, or until the filling is set and slightly puffed, and the crust is golden brown.

Cool and Serve:
- Allow the pie to cool completely on a wire rack before slicing and serving.
- Serve slices of the Thai Tea Pecan Pie on its own or with a dollop of whipped cream or a scoop of vanilla ice cream, if desired.

Enjoy:
- Enjoy the rich and flavorful Thai Tea Pecan Pie as a delightful dessert, perfect for any occasion!

This Thai Tea Pecan Pie offers a unique twist on the classic pecan pie, with the addition of aromatic Thai tea flavors. It's sure to be a hit with family and friends!

Thai Tea Bundt Cake

Ingredients:

For the cake:

- 2 cups all-purpose flour
- 2 tablespoons Thai tea leaves
- 1 teaspoon baking powder
- 1/2 teaspoon baking soda
- 1/4 teaspoon salt
- 1 cup unsalted butter, softened
- 1 1/2 cups granulated sugar
- 4 large eggs
- 1 teaspoon vanilla extract
- 1/2 cup buttermilk, at room temperature

For the glaze:

- 1 cup powdered sugar
- 2-3 tablespoons brewed Thai tea, cooled
- 1/2 teaspoon vanilla extract

Instructions:

Prepare the Thai Tea Infusion:
- In a small saucepan, heat the buttermilk until it just begins to steam. Add the Thai tea leaves and let them steep for 10-15 minutes. Strain the buttermilk to remove the tea leaves and set aside to cool.

Make the Cake:
- Preheat the oven to 350°F (175°C). Grease and flour a 10-cup Bundt pan.
- In a mixing bowl, sift together the flour, baking powder, baking soda, and salt. Set aside.
- In a large mixing bowl, cream together the softened butter and granulated sugar until light and fluffy.
- Beat in the eggs, one at a time, until well combined. Stir in the vanilla extract.

- Gradually add the dry ingredients to the wet ingredients, alternating with the cooled Thai tea-infused buttermilk, beginning and ending with the dry ingredients. Mix until just combined.
- Pour the batter into the prepared Bundt pan and smooth the top with a spatula.
- Bake for 45-55 minutes, or until a toothpick inserted into the center of the cake comes out clean.
- Remove the cake from the oven and let it cool in the pan for 10 minutes before transferring it to a wire rack to cool completely.

Make the Glaze:
- In a small bowl, whisk together the powdered sugar, brewed Thai tea, and vanilla extract until smooth.

Glaze the Cake:
- Once the cake has cooled completely, drizzle the glaze over the top of the cake, allowing it to drip down the sides.

Serve:
- Slice and serve the Thai Tea Bundt Cake and enjoy its delightful flavor and moist texture!

This Thai Tea Bundt Cake is sure to impress with its unique flavor and beautiful presentation. It's perfect for serving at special occasions or enjoying as a delicious treat any time!

Thai Tea Fudge

Ingredients:

- 2 cups white chocolate chips
- 1 (14 oz) can sweetened condensed milk
- 2 tablespoons Thai tea leaves
- 1/4 cup unsalted butter
- 1 teaspoon vanilla extract
- Pinch of salt
- Optional: Chopped nuts or shredded coconut for topping

Instructions:

Prepare Thai Tea Infusion:
- In a small saucepan, heat the sweetened condensed milk over low heat until it starts to steam. Add the Thai tea leaves and let them steep for 10-15 minutes. Strain the milk to remove the tea leaves and set aside.

Melt White Chocolate:
- In a microwave-safe bowl, combine the white chocolate chips and butter. Microwave in 30-second intervals, stirring in between, until the chocolate and butter are melted and smooth.

Combine Ingredients:
- Stir the Thai tea-infused sweetened condensed milk into the melted white chocolate mixture until well combined.
- Add the vanilla extract and a pinch of salt, stirring until incorporated.

Pour into Pan:
- Line an 8x8 inch baking pan with parchment paper or aluminum foil, leaving some overhang for easy removal.
- Pour the fudge mixture into the prepared pan, spreading it out evenly with a spatula.

Optional Toppings:
- If desired, sprinkle chopped nuts or shredded coconut over the top of the fudge and gently press them down.

Chill:
- Place the pan in the refrigerator and chill the fudge for at least 2-3 hours, or until set.

Slice and Serve:

- Once the fudge is set, use the parchment paper or foil overhang to lift it out of the pan. Place it on a cutting board and slice it into squares.

Enjoy:
- Serve the Thai Tea Fudge and enjoy its rich and creamy texture with aromatic Thai tea flavor!

This Thai Tea Fudge makes a delightful treat for any occasion. Enjoy it as a delicious dessert or package it up for a thoughtful homemade gift!

Thai Tea Baklava

Ingredients:

For the baklava:

- 1 package (16 oz) phyllo dough, thawed according to package instructions
- 1 cup unsalted butter, melted
- 2 cups finely ground almonds or walnuts
- 1/4 cup Thai tea leaves
- 1/2 cup granulated sugar
- 1 teaspoon ground cinnamon

For the honey syrup:

- 1 cup water
- 1 cup granulated sugar
- 1/2 cup honey
- 2 tablespoons fresh lemon juice
- 1 cinnamon stick
- 2-3 tablespoons brewed Thai tea, cooled

Instructions:

Prepare the Thai Tea Infusion:
- In a small saucepan, heat 2 cups of water until it begins to steam. Add the Thai tea leaves and let them steep for 10-15 minutes. Strain the tea to remove the leaves and set aside to cool.

Make the Honey Syrup:
- In a saucepan, combine the water, granulated sugar, honey, lemon juice, and cinnamon stick. Bring to a boil over medium heat, stirring until the sugar is dissolved.
- Reduce the heat to low and simmer for 10-15 minutes, until the syrup thickens slightly.
- Remove from heat and stir in the brewed Thai tea. Allow the syrup to cool completely, then discard the cinnamon stick.

Prepare the Baklava Filling:

- In a mixing bowl, combine the finely ground almonds or walnuts with the granulated sugar and ground cinnamon. Set aside.

Assemble the Baklava:
- Preheat the oven to 350°F (175°C). Lightly grease a 9x13 inch baking dish.
- Place one sheet of phyllo dough in the bottom of the prepared baking dish, brushing it lightly with melted butter. Repeat with 7-8 more sheets of phyllo dough, brushing each layer with butter.
- Sprinkle a thin, even layer of the nut mixture over the phyllo dough.
- Continue layering phyllo dough and nut mixture, brushing each layer of dough with butter, until all of the nut mixture is used.
- Finish with a final layer of phyllo dough, brushing the top generously with butter.

Cut and Bake:
- Use a sharp knife to cut the baklava into diamond or square shapes.
- Bake in the preheated oven for 45-50 minutes, or until the baklava is golden brown and crisp.

Pour the Syrup:
- Once the baklava is done baking, remove it from the oven and immediately pour the cooled honey syrup over the hot baklava, making sure to cover it evenly.
- Allow the baklava to cool completely in the pan, allowing the syrup to soak in.

Serve:
- Once cooled, serve the Thai Tea Baklava and enjoy its unique flavor and crunchy texture.

This Thai Tea Baklava offers a delightful fusion of Middle Eastern and Thai flavors, making it a memorable dessert for any occasion. Enjoy it with a cup of brewed Thai tea for a perfect pairing!

Thai Tea Éclair

Ingredients:

For the éclair shells:

- 1/2 cup unsalted butter
- 1 cup water
- 1 cup all-purpose flour
- 4 large eggs

For the Thai tea pastry cream:

- 1 cup whole milk
- 2 tablespoons Thai tea leaves
- 3 large egg yolks
- 1/4 cup granulated sugar
- 2 tablespoons cornstarch
- 1 teaspoon vanilla extract
- Pinch of salt

For the glaze:

- 1 cup powdered sugar
- 2-3 tablespoons brewed Thai tea, cooled
- 1/2 teaspoon vanilla extract

Instructions:

Prepare the Éclair Shells:
- Preheat the oven to 400°F (200°C). Line a baking sheet with parchment paper.
- In a medium saucepan, combine the butter and water. Bring to a boil over medium heat.
- Add the flour all at once and stir vigorously until the mixture forms a smooth ball of dough that pulls away from the sides of the pan.
- Remove the pan from the heat and let the dough cool for a few minutes.

- Add the eggs, one at a time, beating well after each addition until the dough is smooth and glossy.
- Transfer the dough to a piping bag fitted with a large round tip. Pipe the dough onto the prepared baking sheet into éclair shapes, about 4 inches long and 1 inch wide.
- Bake for 15 minutes, then reduce the oven temperature to 350°F (175°C) and continue baking for an additional 20-25 minutes, or until the éclairs are golden brown and puffed. Remove from the oven and let them cool completely on a wire rack.

Prepare the Thai Tea Pastry Cream:
- In a small saucepan, heat the milk until it just begins to steam. Add the Thai tea leaves and let them steep for 10-15 minutes. Strain the milk to remove the tea leaves and return it to the saucepan.
- In a mixing bowl, whisk together the egg yolks, granulated sugar, cornstarch, and salt until well combined.
- Gradually whisk the warm Thai tea-infused milk into the egg yolk mixture until smooth.
- Pour the mixture back into the saucepan and cook over medium heat, stirring constantly, until the pastry cream thickens and comes to a boil.
- Remove from heat and stir in the vanilla extract. Transfer the pastry cream to a bowl and cover it with plastic wrap, pressing the wrap directly onto the surface of the pastry cream to prevent a skin from forming. Refrigerate until chilled.

Fill the Éclairs:
- Once the éclair shells and pastry cream are cooled, use a sharp knife to slice each éclair shell in half horizontally.
- Spoon or pipe the chilled pastry cream into the bottom half of each éclair shell. Replace the top half.

Make the Glaze:
- In a small bowl, whisk together the powdered sugar, brewed Thai tea, and vanilla extract until smooth.

Glaze the Éclairs:
- Dip the top of each filled éclair into the glaze, allowing any excess to drip off. Place the glazed éclairs on a wire rack set over a baking sheet to catch any drips.

Chill and Serve:
- Chill the glazed éclairs in the refrigerator for about 30 minutes to allow the glaze to set.

- Serve the Thai Tea Éclairs chilled and enjoy their delicious flavor and creamy filling!

These Thai Tea Éclairs are sure to impress with their unique flavor and elegant appearance. They're perfect for special occasions or as a delightful treat any time!

Thai Tea Biscotti

Ingredients:

- 2 cups all-purpose flour
- 1 teaspoon baking powder
- 1/4 teaspoon salt
- 1/2 cup granulated sugar
- 1/4 cup unsalted butter, softened
- 2 large eggs
- 2 tablespoons Thai tea leaves
- 1 teaspoon vanilla extract
- 1/2 cup chopped almonds or pecans (optional)
- Zest of 1 orange (optional)

Instructions:

Prepare Thai Tea Infusion:
- In a small saucepan, heat 1/2 cup of water until it begins to steam. Add the Thai tea leaves and let them steep for 10-15 minutes. Strain the tea to remove the leaves and set aside to cool.

Preheat Oven and Prepare Baking Sheet:
- Preheat your oven to 350°F (175°C). Line a baking sheet with parchment paper or a silicone baking mat.

Make the Biscotti Dough:
- In a mixing bowl, sift together the flour, baking powder, and salt.
- In another mixing bowl, cream together the softened butter and granulated sugar until light and fluffy.
- Beat in the eggs, one at a time, until well combined.
- Stir in the cooled Thai tea infusion and vanilla extract until incorporated.
- Gradually add the dry ingredients to the wet ingredients, mixing until a dough forms.
- If desired, mix in chopped nuts and orange zest until evenly distributed throughout the dough.

Shape the Biscotti Logs:
- Divide the dough in half. On a lightly floured surface, shape each half into a log about 12 inches long and 2 inches wide. Place the logs on the prepared baking sheet, spacing them apart.

Bake the Biscotti Logs:
- Bake the logs in the preheated oven for 25-30 minutes, or until firm and lightly golden brown.

Cool and Slice:
- Remove the baked logs from the oven and let them cool on the baking sheet for about 10 minutes.
- Using a serrated knife, slice the logs diagonally into 1/2-inch thick slices.

Second Bake:
- Arrange the biscotti slices cut side down on the baking sheet.
- Return the biscotti to the oven and bake for an additional 10-15 minutes, or until the biscotti are golden brown and crisp.

Cool and Serve:
- Once baked, let the biscotti cool completely on a wire rack.
- Serve the Thai Tea Biscotti with your favorite hot or cold beverage and enjoy the crunchy texture and delightful Thai tea flavor!

These Thai Tea Biscotti are perfect for dunking into coffee, tea, or milk, and they also make lovely gifts when packaged in decorative bags or boxes. Enjoy their unique flavor and crunchy texture any time of day!

Thai Tea Crêpes Suzette

Ingredients:

For the crêpes:

- 1 cup all-purpose flour
- 2 large eggs
- 1 cup milk
- 1/4 cup brewed Thai tea, cooled
- 2 tablespoons granulated sugar
- 2 tablespoons unsalted butter, melted
- 1/4 teaspoon salt
- Additional butter or oil for cooking

For the orange sauce:

- Zest and juice of 2 oranges
- Zest and juice of 1 lemon
- 1/2 cup granulated sugar
- 1/4 cup unsalted butter
- 1/4 cup Grand Marnier or orange liqueur
- 2 tablespoons brewed Thai tea, cooled

For serving (optional):

- Vanilla ice cream or whipped cream
- Additional orange zest for garnish
- Fresh mint leaves for garnish

Instructions:

Prepare the Crêpe Batter:
- In a mixing bowl, whisk together the flour, eggs, milk, brewed Thai tea, sugar, melted butter, and salt until smooth and well combined. Let the batter rest for 15-30 minutes.

Cook the Crêpes:

- Heat a non-stick skillet or crêpe pan over medium heat and lightly grease it with butter or oil.
- Pour about 1/4 cup of the crêpe batter into the hot skillet, swirling it around to evenly coat the bottom. Cook for 1-2 minutes until the edges start to lift and the bottom is lightly golden. Flip the crêpe and cook for another 1-2 minutes on the other side. Repeat with the remaining batter, stacking the cooked crêpes on a plate.

Prepare the Orange Sauce:
- In a large skillet or saucepan, combine the orange zest, lemon zest, orange juice, lemon juice, sugar, and unsalted butter. Cook over medium heat, stirring occasionally, until the sugar has dissolved and the mixture begins to simmer.
- Reduce the heat to low and let the sauce simmer for about 5 minutes until slightly thickened.
- Stir in the Grand Marnier and brewed Thai tea, and simmer for another 2-3 minutes. Remove the sauce from heat and set aside.

Assemble the Crêpes Suzette:
- Fold each crêpe into quarters and place them in the orange sauce in the skillet, arranging them in a single layer.
- Spoon some of the sauce over the crêpes and let them soak for a minute or two.

Serve:
- Serve the Thai Tea Crêpes Suzette warm, drizzled with additional orange sauce.
- Optionally, top each serving with a scoop of vanilla ice cream or whipped cream, and garnish with fresh orange zest and mint leaves.

Enjoy:
- Enjoy the luscious Thai Tea Crêpes Suzette, savoring the harmonious blend of citrusy orange flavors with the aromatic notes of Thai tea, complemented by the delicate texture of the crêpes.

This elegant dessert is perfect for special occasions or whenever you crave a decadent treat with a touch of exotic flair.

Thai Tea Brulee Cheesecake

Ingredients:

For the crust:

- 1 1/2 cups graham cracker crumbs
- 1/4 cup granulated sugar
- 1/2 cup unsalted butter, melted

For the cheesecake filling:

- 3 packages (24 oz total) cream cheese, softened
- 1 cup granulated sugar
- 3 large eggs
- 1/4 cup brewed Thai tea, cooled
- 1 teaspoon vanilla extract
- 1 tablespoon all-purpose flour

For the brûlée topping:

- 1/2 cup granulated sugar (for caramelizing)

Instructions:

Preheat the Oven:
- Preheat your oven to 325°F (160°C). Grease a 9-inch springform pan and wrap the bottom of the pan with aluminum foil to prevent any leakage.

Make the Crust:
- In a mixing bowl, combine the graham cracker crumbs, granulated sugar, and melted butter. Press the mixture evenly into the bottom of the prepared springform pan. Use the bottom of a glass to press it down firmly.
- Bake the crust in the preheated oven for 10 minutes. Remove from the oven and let it cool while you prepare the cheesecake filling.

Prepare the Cheesecake Filling:

- In a large mixing bowl, beat the softened cream cheese and granulated sugar until smooth and creamy.
- Add the eggs one at a time, beating well after each addition.
- Stir in the brewed Thai tea, vanilla extract, and flour until well combined and smooth.
- Pour the cheesecake filling over the baked crust in the springform pan.

Bake the Cheesecake:
- Place the springform pan in a large roasting pan. Carefully pour hot water into the roasting pan to create a water bath around the springform pan, about halfway up the sides.
- Bake the cheesecake in the preheated oven for 55-60 minutes, or until the edges are set and the center is slightly jiggly.
- Turn off the oven and let the cheesecake cool gradually in the oven with the door closed for about 1 hour.

Chill the Cheesecake:
- Remove the cheesecake from the oven and let it cool completely at room temperature. Then cover it with plastic wrap and refrigerate for at least 4 hours or overnight until thoroughly chilled and set.

Brûlée the Cheesecake:
- Before serving, sprinkle the top of the chilled cheesecake evenly with granulated sugar.
- Use a kitchen torch to caramelize the sugar until it forms a golden brown crust. Alternatively, you can place the cheesecake under the broiler for a few minutes until the sugar caramelizes.
- Let the caramelized sugar cool and harden before slicing and serving the Thai Tea Brûlée Cheesecake.

Serve and Enjoy:
- Slice the cheesecake into wedges and serve it chilled. Enjoy the creamy texture, rich Thai tea flavor, and crunchy brûlée topping!

This Thai Tea Brûlée Cheesecake is sure to impress with its decadent combination of creamy cheesecake and caramelized sweetness, accented by the exotic notes of Thai tea. It's perfect for special occasions or whenever you crave a luxurious dessert experience.

www.ingramcontent.com/pod-product-compliance
Lightning Source LLC
LaVergne TN
LVHW061940070526
838199LV00060B/3899